SURVIVAL ON A WESTWARD TREK

SURVIVAL ON
A WESTWARD TREK
1858–1859

The John Jones Overlanders

* * *

Dwight L. Smith

OHIO UNIVERSITY PRESS Athens

Library of Congress Cataloging-in-Publication Data
Jones, John, fl. 1858–1859.
  Survival on a westward trek, 1858–1859 : the John Jones
overlanders / [edited by] Dwight L. Smith.
    p.   cm.
  Bibliography: p.
  Includes index.
  ISBN 0-8214-0921-2
    1. Overland journeys to the Pacific. 2. Canada, Western—
Description and travel. 3. Jones, John, fl. 1858–1859—Diaries.
4. British Columbia—Gold discoveries. 5. Fraser River Region
(B.C.)—Gold discoveries. I. Smith, Dwight La Vern, 1918– .
II. Title.
F1060.8.J66   1989
978'.02—dc19   89-31053 CIP

To Jane, Greg, and Becki

C O N T E N T S

I L L U S T R A T I O N S

PREFACE

John W. Jones, a restless young man who never seemed to settle down, was working as a clerk in a public office in Chatfield, Minnesota Territory, when the newspapers began to report the discovery of gold in British Columbia. Jones joined with several others who had caught the fever and headed for the goldfields by way of the fur trade routes across the Canadian prairies.

Overlanders, as such persons are referred to in Canadian history, were never very numerous. The peak of trans-prairie gold rushers was in 1862, and only a few of these left accounts of their journeys. There are vague references made to overlanders as early as 1858, but the literature lacks any substantial accounts of activity for that year.

Given these circumstances, the Jones journal of the 1858–1859 trek of his party stands as the earliest detailed record of those who pursued their dream by crossing the continent. Never before published, Lawrence W. Towner, former President and Librarian, Newberry Library, and James M. Wells, former Vice President, Newberry Library, granted permission and encouraged me to prepare a critical rendering of the Jones journal for publication.

A Summer Research Appointment from Miami University, appointment as Fellow, Huntington Library, San Marino, California, and a Research Grant from the Department of Intergovernmental Affairs, Province of Quebec, enabled me to conduct the fine-tooth-comb research necessary to ferret out the fugitive materials related to this project.

The staffs of widely located libraries, museums, and archives answered queries and made their resources available to me. In Quebec: McGill University Library, Montreal. In Minnesota: Minnesota Historical Society, St. Paul; University of Minnesota Library, Minneapolis. In Manitoba: Hudson's Bay Company Archives, Winnipeg; Manitoba Historical Society, Winnipeg; Manitoba Museum of Man and Nature, Winnipeg; Manitoba Provincial Library, Winnipeg; Manitoba Provincial Archives, Winnipeg.

In Saskatchewan: University of Regina Library, Regina; Saskatchewan Provincial Library, Regina; Regina Public Library, Regina; Provincial Archives of Saskatchewan, Regina and Saskatoon; University of Saskatchewan Archives and Special Collections, Saskatoon. In Alberta: Provincial Archives of Alberta, Edmonton; Edmonton Municipal Archives; Glenbow Archives, Calgary; University of Calgary Library, Calgary. In British Columbia: Vernon Museum, Vernon; Kamloops Museum, Kamloops; Yale and District Society Museum, Yale; University of British Columbia Library, Vancouver; Provincial Archives of British Columbia, Victoria.

In Washington: Washington State Historical Society, Tacoma; Washington State Library, Olympia. In Oregon: Oregon State Historical Society, Portland; Fort Dalles Museum, The Dalles; Wasco County-Dalles City Library, The Dalles. In California: Huntington Library, San Marino. In Indiana: Indiana University Library, Bloomington. In Ohio: Miami University Libraries, Oxford.

I wish to single out certain persons who have helped in specialized and particular ways to enhance my research efforts: Ron Walrath, Curator of Newspapers, Minnesota Historical Society, St. Paul; Judith Hudson Beattie, Head, Research and Reference, Hudson's Bay Company Archives, Provincial Archives of Manitoba, Winnipeg; Nancy J. Moeckel, Science

Library, Miami University, Oxford, Ohio; William C. Pratt, Department of English, Miami University; Benjamin F. Plybon, Department of Mathematics and Statistics, Miami University; Sarah C. Barr and Karen S. Clift, Interlibrary Loan Division, Miami University Libraries.

My wife, Jane D. Smith, has consistently supported my efforts all through this project. And she has once more demonstrated her uncanny knack for proofreading, ferreting out those embarrassments that somehow manage to persist or to creep into one's manuscript even in its final stages.

INTRODUCTION

On 6 May 1859, *The Dalles* (Oregon) *Journal* reported the arrival of an overland party from Minnesota. A rather unusual journey had thus come to an unanticipated conclusion. The destination for the trek was beyond their reach. Adjustment to the vagaries of climate and terrain replaced their goal with the priority of survival. The beck and call of the goldfields gave way to whatever safe haven they could make their way. The saga of the John Jones overlanders is the first-hand account of their shattered dreams.[1]

Whenever and wherever gold is discovered, news travels rapidly. While major finds and big rushes were given much attention, even the lesser and insignificant ones were usually reported by newspapers far and wide. It is not surprising, for example, that Canadian papers would carry lengthy accounts of gold discoveries in Iowa, each obtaining their information from different Iowa papers.[2]

---

[1] The first Minnesota newspaper to reprint this news was the *Chatfield Democrat*, 18 June 1859. It was followed by the *Faribault Central Republican*, 22 June 1859, and *St. Paul Daily Pioneer and Democrat*, 25 June 1859.

[2] *Montreal* (Quebec) *Argus*, 13 April 1858; *Toronto* (Ontario) *Globe*, 28 May 1858.

Other accounts noted discoveries and mining activities in such places as Pikes Peak, Arizona, Sonora, and Australia. *Toronto Globe*, 12, 14, 18 June, 6, 9, 14 October, 24, 25, 29 November, 4 December 1858.

In the spring of 1858, word reached the outside world that gold was to be found in abundance in the Fraser River country of British Columbia. Fever spread down along the Pacific coast and thousands of Californians scrambled to find sailing vessels and steamers to take them there. Others from the interior began to make their way overland.[3]

In only as much time as it took ships to carry the news and sometimes gold dust from the west coast, newspapers in New York and other east coast ports were proclaiming and editorializing on the exciting course of events. An occasional letter to an eastern relative or acquaintance, printed in the newspapers, added credence to the exciting news. It was not long before newspaper correspondents began to furnish more systematic coverage of the developments. Such news, of course, soon reached Europe and received similar journalistic treatment there too.

Before there were telegraph and wire services to disseminate news to subscribing newspapers as they do today, newspapers in the mid-nineteenth century simply copied from each other. By this surprisingly efficient means, the story of the Fraser rush spread from eastern papers westward into the interior of the continent. By early May in Toronto and Montreal readers were getting the news from New York and London newspapers and occasionally from other sources.[4] Interest was more than casual since the excitement was taking place in British North American territory, and since Manifest Destiny was giving Ameri-

[3] For a concise account of the Fraser River gold rush see Margaret A. Ormsby, *British Columbia: A History* (Toronto: The Macmillans in Canada, 1958), pp. 138–182. See also Frederic W. Howay, *The Early History of the Fraser River Mines,* Archives of British Columbia, Memoir No. 6 (Victoria, British Columbia: Provincial Library, 1926).

[4] *Toronto Globe,* 3, 4 May 1858, et passim; *Montreal Argus,* 26 May 1858, et passim. Confirmed good news and bad news, rumors, speculations, and encouraging and discouraging commentary, from whatever sources they could be obtained, kept readers reasonably well informed of gold-related developments on the other side of the continent. For an example of exaggerated hyperbole see *Toronto Globe,* 19 July 1858, reprinting from a London, England, paper.

cans voracious appetites for as much of the continent as they could grab.

As elsewhere, Canadians too were susceptible to goldfever and might decide to seek their fortunes in the Fraser goldfields. Getting there by ocean steamer from New York to Panama, trans-Isthmus of Panama railroad, steamer to British Columbia, and then overland up the Fraser River seemed too expensive and too unnecessarily long a journey. Some began to speculate about going overland, perhaps utilizing rivers and lakes en route. Canadians were reminded that "As most of our readers are aware, it is perfectly possible for a person entering a canoe at Toronto to float it, without any other aid than the labour of two men, [and utilizing a few portages,] into the Pacific Ocean."[5]

The Fraser gold rush and related matters continued to receive considerable attention in 1858. Since there was little said specifically about Canadians themselves going to the goldfields, however, it is a reasonable conclusion that not many went that year. A Buffalo correspondent "late of England," to a Toronto paper, representing "a company of young men, now made up to about forty, which we hope to increase to one hundred," asked about trouble in crossing Hudson's Bay Company lands; but nothing else was reported about that projected overland venture.[6] A Toronto meeting was called to consider formation of a "Vancouver's Island and Fraser's River Emigration Society." A constitution was formulated and membership offered. If anything further developed within the year, the newspaper was silent on the matter.[7]

---

[5] *Toronto Globe,* 15, 24 May 1858; *Montreal Argus,* 26 May 1858. The 24 May *Globe* account was reprinted and editorialized for British Columbia readers under the headline "Immigration Hither from Canada," *Victoria Gazette,* 17 July 1858.

[6] *Toronto Globe,* 7 June 1858.

[7] Ibid., 7, 10, 30, 31 July 1858.

A brief statement of "several young men" from Galt who expected to leave shortly was the only other report made in the paper in 1858. Ibid., 27 August 1858.

The Canadian press may have been more prescient than it realized about the lure of the news of the Fraser gold rush of 1858 on the Canadians or it simply may have been speaking with caution and wisdom: "Doubtless there is much gold in Canada . . . but our hardy population are not in such haste to be rich as to leave their farms untilled for the purpose of digging for gold, . . . the natural temperament of Canadians lead them to value higher the gold obtained from the cultivation of the soil and the prosecution of mercantile pursuits and useful arts, than by seeking for it in a mine in all its virgin purity."[8]

*   *   *

Be that as it may, the Canadian newspapers began to pick up another facet of the gold rush, a matter of increasing concern. From time to time they discussed the merits of a sea or an overland route to the Fraser mines. The comment that the overland journey could move "either by the Canadian route through Lake Superior or by St. Paul, and then over the plains" expresses the concern succinctly.[9] The key words here are "by St. Paul."

The circumstances of geography, transportation, and settlement made it difficult to go from the St. Lawrence Valley north around the Great Lakes to the western prairies of Canada. At the same time, it was becoming easier and more practical to make the east to west traverse by moving through American territory south of the Great Lakes and re-entering British territory by way of St. Paul and the Red River and on to the Red River settlement at Fort Garry in present southern Manitoba.

By the mid-century years the maturing Minnesota Territory was aspiring to statehood. The Red River settlement's principal lifeline to the outside world was shifting from a northward

[8] *Montreal Argus,* 29 June 1858.
[9] *Toronto Globe,* 24 May 1858; *Montreal Argus,* 26 May 1858; *Victoria Gazette,* 17 July 1858.

connection with Hudson Bay to a southward orientation. Its commerce and mail, as well as that of the Hudson's Bay Company, was coming principally by way of the Red River and St. Paul, Minnesota.

Settlement in the United States had moved westward into the Mississippi Valley. Manifest Destiny was pushing political boundaries on to the Pacific Coast, and the far western areas were developing rapidly. Gold rushers, settlers, and others began to cross the continent. To accommodate this development and to establish lines of communication, private as well as governmental surveys and speculations projected the establishment of wagon roads, water routes, and railroads to connect the Mississippi Valley and the Far West.

Minnesotans were strategically situated for such connections to the Far West on either side of the international border. The Fraser gold rush heightened their interest in the potential of St. Paul becoming the gateway to the Canadian prairies both for settlement and as the point of departure for the gold fields. This went beyond idle speculation. Not only did public meetings and the press talk about it, but the legislature of the new (11 May 1858) state even appointed a "Select Committee on Overland Route to British Oregon."[10]

The Canadian press picked up these developments from the Minnesota papers, watched them closely, and reported and commented on them with as much diligence as with information gleaned from New York and other papers about the gold

[10] Minnesota Legislature, House, Select Committee on Overland Route to British Oregon, *Report,* 1st Leg., 1st sess., 1858; Alvin C. Gluek, Jr., *Minnesota and the Manifest Destiny of the Canadian Northwest: A Study in Canadian American Relations* (Toronto: University of Toronto Press, 1965), pp. 93–157; Alvin C. Gluek, Jr., "The Minnesota Route," *Beaver* Outfit 286 (Spring 1956): 44–50; W. L. Morton, *The Kingdom of Canada: A General History from Earliest Times,* 2d ed. (Toronto: McClelland and Stewart, 1969), pp. 299–302; *Toronto Globe,* 9 September 1858. Several Minnesota newspapers reported these developments, for example, *Saint Paul Daily Minnesotian,* 2, 9, 24, 28 July, 13, 14 August, 1858; *Saint Paul Weekly Minnesotian,* 3, 10, 31 July, 14, 21 August 1858.

rush itself. "The Americans are fully alive to the importance of the late gold discoveries at Fraser's river, and ere long thousands of people from other states than California will be wending their way to the new El Dorado."[11] A week after this, a Toronto editor predicted that "active measures will undoubtedly be taken, and that with as little delay as possible to establish an overland communication" with the Fraser River mines.[12] Soon "several [Minnesota] parties" were reported preparing to depart for the gold country.[13]

* * *

The Fraser River developments gave further impetus to the westward dreaming and planning of Minnesotans. That the aborning state aspired to transportation and communication connections with the West on either side of the international boundary was a given assumption of surveys, public meetings, and editorials. Added focus to the Canadian route now received particular attention as it was expected that the gold-fields would become the principal destination of westward bound travelers and freight.[14]

Some Minnesotans did succumb to the fever in 1858 and started out overland to seek their fortune. It is curious, however, that only comparatively few, as reported by the press, decided to make the journey. It is further interesting that, except for one party, little was reported about the identity and the progress of these would-be gold rushers. A plausible conclusion is that few actually started on the trek and that fewer of these traveled very far.[15]

---

[11] *Toronto Globe*, 12 July 1858. Similar apprehensiveness was noted in the reprint in Manchester, England, and Glasgow papers. Ibid., 21 July 1858.

[12] Ibid., 19, 21 July 1858. The public meetings in St. Paul were given full coverage. Ibid., 28, 30, 31 July 1858.

[13] Ibid., 2, 17 August 1858.

[14] The Minnesota newspapers reported these developments and disseminated whatever news could be found in New York papers.

[15] The *St. Paul Daily Pioneer and Democrat* is the principal source of information on these developments. Others carried some news. And they all borrowed

The term "overlanders" applies in the broadest sense to explorers, migration parties, and others who crossed the Canadian prairies. It has been used more specifically as a label by Mark Sweeten Wade particularly for those enticed by the lure of gold in British Columbia. He gave currency to this application of the term in his account, *The Overlanders of '62*, distinguishing them from those whose ultimate western destination was the Oregon country south of the 49th parallel. Wade included brief accounts of three 1859 parties with the Fraser River mines as their goal, but his emphasis was on 1862.[16]

Additional documentation of the overlanders of 1862 has been added to the literature of the British Columbia gold rushes; but little of a substantive nature has been found about the 1859 overlanders beyond what Wade reported.[17]

*   *   *

or reprinted from each other. This makes it probable that not too much is lost from the fact that surviving files of the newspapers have scattered gaps in them.

Occasional reference is made to some gold fever victims who planned to go to the Selkirk settlement for the winter and to proceed westward in the spring. See, for example, *Saint Paul Weekly Minnesotian*, 20 August 1858.

[16] Mark Sweeten Wade, *The Overlanders of '62*, Archives of British Columbia, no. 9 (Victoria, British Columbia: Printed by Charles F. Banfield, 1931), pp. 1–9; Ralph C. Russell, *The Carlton Trail: The Broad Highway into the Saskatchewan Country from the Red River Settlement, 1840–1880* (Saskatoon, Saskatchewan: Modern Press, 1956), p. 31.

The literature of overlanders, in the larger sense of the term, is discussed in Victor G. Hopwood, "Explorers by Land to 1867," in *Literary History of Canada: Canadian Literature in English*, ed. Carl F. Klinck et al., 3 vols., 2d ed. (Toronto: University of Toronto Press, 1976), chapter 2.

[17] The paucity of documentation makes it impossible to determine how many overlanders there were in the 1859–1862 years. For a brief discussion which arrives at a reasonable estimate of two hundred, see Victor G. Hopwood's introduction to Margaret McNaughton, *Overland to Cariboo: An Eventful Journey of Canadian Pioneers to the Gold Fields of British Columbia in 1862* (Vancouver, British Columbia: J. J. Douglas, 1973).

Except for the contemporary record itself, virtually nothing has been said about the 1858 overlanders. Although the evidence that Canadians and Americans sought to reach the Fraser River country by traveling overland across western Canada that year is fugitive, it is sufficient to establish the fact. To the present at least, beyond scattered references to others in newspapers, the John W. Jones journal is the only substantial documentation of the record for 1858.[18]

The excitement caused by the news of the gold discovery and rush in British Columbia being reported in the Minnesota newspapers gave further impetus to the immediate and potential significance of prairie Canada, especially if Minnesota was going to establish communication and transportation connections with the Pacific coast. Public meetings discussed such things as possible routes, the agricultural potential of the prairies for settlement, and whether these could be realized better if the area was brought under American jurisdiction.

Several Faribault, Minnesota, men decided to travel overland across western Canada to seek their fortune in the Fraser goldfields.[19] Organized into two messes, one of five men, and four in the other, they loaded their wagons, and, with a festive send-off, left on 20 July 1858 for St. Paul, the Red River, and British America. They viewed their prospects in a spirit of adventure and with a feeling of optimism. Reaching the goldfields would pose no particular problems or hardships because there were well-established trade routes from St. Paul to the Red River settlements of southern Manitoba. After that, long-

[18] An example of the fugitive nature of this documentation can be found in a letter of one trekker who, as does Jones, makes occasional reference to others, mentions he was traveling with two others. William Brewster to "Dear Sister," 12 December 1858, William Brewster Correspondence Outward, Provincial Archives of British Columbia, Victoria, British Columbia.

[19] *Faribault Central Republican,* 4 August 1858, 22 June, 6 July 1859; *Mankato* (Minn.) *Weekly Independent,* 16 July 1859; *Saint Paul Daily Minnesotian,* 26 July 1858; *Saint Paul Weekly Minnesotian,* 31 July 1858.

used fur trade trails would take them from post to post of the
Hudson's Bay Company. Even the passes through the Rocky
Mountains were well enough known to get them into the
hinterlands of British Columbia. Previous experiences of some
of their party on survey and exploring expeditions would stand
them in good stead. There was game and grass to sustain man
and beast on the trek. Not all Indians were friendly to be sure,
but this was a necessary risk they had to take.

The Jones party picked up some more supplies, equipment,
and information at St. Paul and struck out northwestward
on the Metropolitan Trail, approximating the course of the
Mississippi River to St. Cloud. In the same general direction
they continued across Minnesota on the Old Middle Trail to
Breckenridge on the Red River boundary between Minnesota
and southeastern North Dakota. Crossing the river they were
now on the River Trail which they hoped to follow all the way
into British territory. They were beginning to add buffalo
hunting, chance meetings with Red River freighting parties,
fear of encounters with Indians, and getting lost to their experiences. Finally crossing the North Dakota-Manitoba boundary they traveled on what was sometimes called the Pembina
Trail, reaching Fort Garry at present Winnipeg a month after
they had left home.

Trading their horse-drawn wagons for ox-drawn Red River
carts, laying in more supplies, and exchanging pleasantries
and information with the traders and soldiers, Jones and his
companions plunged westward. It was not long before they
passed the last of the scattered settlements and were in the
prairie wilderness. They were on the Carlton Trail, the principal east-west route of the fur traders. Following the Assiniboine River westward from Fort Garry to Fort Ellice near the
mouth of the Qu'Appelle River and the Manitoba-Saskatche-
wan border, the trail then went northwestward to Fort Carlton
on the North Saskatchewan River about fifty miles due north
of Saskatoon. Generally northwestward, approximating the
course of the North Saskatchewan, the trail led them by way

of Fort Pitt near the Saskatchewan-Alberta border and on to Fort Edmonton.

The routine of life on the trail was modified happily and otherwise. Tension mounted between Jones and one of his companions and they almost came to blows. The party became quite adept at fording streams in the skin-boat manner of the country. At Fort Ellice they caught up with an independent trader and his train with whom they traveled to Fort Pitt where the trader left the trail. This was a mutually beneficial and rewarding arrangement. The occasional lack of firewood, a shortage of water, and other things such as the scarcity of game caused some anxiety. Although they tried valiantly, the Minnesotans could not stomach the boiled skunk offered by their trader friend. Starting in mid-September and for a month, they were treated to Donati's comet, a stellar attraction that received worldwide attention and is still given prominent billing in astronomy textbooks. Their pork and beans were quite acceptable contributions to an occasional friendly meal with the Indians or traders. Not all Indians were to be trusted, however, and care was taken against their "thieving propensities."

Before the Faribault party reached Fort Edmonton in mid-October, frosty nights and occasional snow reminded them that the season was getting late. Advised there that once the passes through the Rocky Mountains were closed for the winter by snow they would not be open again until late summer of the next year, Jones and nine of his party decided to press on, using a more southerly pass that would take them into northern Idaho and northeastern Washington and on to the Fraser River country.

Heading south out of Edmonton, probably following the Cart Trail, sometimes called Wolf's Trail, they learned of hostile Indians ahead and deep snow in the pass they had planned to use. Altering their course for another pass, they temporarily lost their way. It is impossible to follow their meanderings. The heavy snow and the cold temperatures made traveling sometimes treacherous; and an uncertain guide did not help much. Finally the party crossed over the North Kootenay Pass and international border and reached the Kootenay trading post, six weeks out of Edmonton.

Except for one of the party who could travel no further because of frozen feet, the others decided to press on for Colville in northeastern Washington, located on a principal route to the gold country of British Columbia. In two weeks of following the trail which approximated the course of the river, they reached an Indian encampment of a dozen lodges at Duck Lake in southern British Columbia.

Three days later their progress became so difficult they concluded their animals would not survive the trip. Four of the men pressed on, hoping to reach Colville on snowshoes. Jones with four companions and their horses turned back to Duck Lake to camp until the snow went off. They built a conical shaped lodge and an eight-by-twelve "shanty" for shelter and joined in the festivities of Christmas and New Years which the Indians had learned from a missionary. After that things were reduced to a dull near-starvation existence for both the Minnesotans and the Indians, with a steady diet of minnows and moss enlivened by occasional meat as their horses began to die. The Indians did not suffer as much only by comparison as these winter circumstances were not unusual for them. Faced with a rapidly diminishing supply of horse meat, Jones and two others decided to strike out on snowshoes for the Colville Valley.

The three left their winter camp on 24 February. After two weeks of difficult traveling and suffering from bleeding feet and waning strength, while climbing up what later proved to be their last range of mountains, Jones gave up, ready to accept death by freezing or starvation. A companion forced him on and later the same day they reached the Colville Valley. A month later Jones had recuperated and was able to move on. For whatever reason, he joined a small party traveling to The Dalles, Oregon, where he arrived in late April.

Jones is silent on the matter, but the Minnesotans had apparently abandoned their goal of joining the Fraser River gold rush and had decided to go their separate ways in pursuit of whatever opportunity they might find.

* * *

Biographically, John W. Jones is elusive. Fugitive references yield only fragmentary information, and some inferences can be drawn from the lack of evidence in other sources. His journal helps a little. The terse "(My birthday.)" in the entry for 7 November is the only vital statistic available. He compared Red River mosquitoes with those he had seen in his previous "travels throughout the different sections of the States, and especially in the swamps of Louisiana and other southern states." This is further explained in part by a newspaper account that said he had been "connected with Capt. R. B. Marcy's exploration of Red River of Louisiana in 1852." In a letter to a Faribault newspaper he referred to the houses of Pembina as "closely resembling the houses of Central America with the exception of the roof," but what he meant by Central America cannot be determined.[20]

He apparently moved to Minnesota sometime after June 1850 as his name is not recorded in the federal census of Minnesota Territory for 1850. For a time, he was a clerk in the office of the Receiver of Public Moneys in Chatfield. From references he made to various persons from Faribault, Jones probably had established residence there prior to the gold rush trek. He identified himself with Faribault and as a Democrat.[21]

[20] Entries for 7 November 1858, 5 August 1858; *Faribault Central Republican,* 4 August, 29 September 1858. The official report of the Marcy expedition does not include rosters of personnel. Randolph B. Marcy, *Exploration of the Red River of Louisiana, in the Year 1852,* 32d Cong., 2 sess., Senate, Executive Doc. No. 54, serial 666, 1853.

[21] United States Department of Commerce, Bureau of the Census, *Seventh Census of the United States, 1850, Minnesota Territory* microfilm roll 367, Record Group 29, National Archives, Washington, D.C.; *St. Paul Pioneer and*

With the final entry of his journal noting his arrival at The Dalles, following Jones once more becomes a problem. On one page in the front of the notebook into which he re-copied the journal he lettered: "J. W. Jones/Portland,/ Oregon." His entry for 19 August 1858 furnishes a clue for dating his presence in Portland. "At this time they [the Red River settlement] had no press; but now as I am copying my old journal . . . I have been informed that the light of the 'Press' has dawned upon them." The *Nor'Wester* was established 28 December 1859. He may have departed from Oregon by 1 June 1860, at least Wasco County (The Dalles) or Multnomah County (Portland), as his name is not recorded in the federal census for 1860.[22]

His immediate whereabouts after this remain a mystery. By whatever route or circumstance, Jones made his way to Austin, Lander County, Nevada. Four clippings pasted into his notebook give the clue for this. They laud his penmanship and orderliness in maintaining the county records in his capacity as "Chief Clerk," and the efficient and friendly manner in which he conducted the business of the clerk's office. Two other clippings praise his design of a pin and the membership roll for the Austin Masonic lodge. The inference can be drawn from a vague reference in his journal that Jones had been a Mason while he was still in Minnesota: "I lost my splendid meerschaum, a gift of Bro. H. D. Bristol, lawyer, a man endeared to me not only by association as a

---

Democrat, 25 June 1859; *Chatfield Democrat,* 18 June, 2 July 1859; entries of 20, 24, 25 July 1858; roster of the party completing the journey, appended to the journal.

[22] Arthur S. Morton, *A History of the Canadian West to 1870–71: Being a History of Rupert's Land (The Hudson's Bay Company's Territory) and of the North-west Territory (Including the Pacific Slope)* (London: Thomas Nelson & Sons, [1939]), pp. 837, 855; United States Department of Commerce, Bureau of the Census, *Eighth Census of the United States, 1860, Multnomah County; Wasco County, Oregon* microfilm roll 1056, Record Group 29, National Archives, Washington, D.C.

foster brother, but by more and worthy motives—that of the 'mystic tie.' "[23]

Silver was discovered in May 1862 in the Reese River country of north central Nevada and a new rush was on. In a few months Lander County was created and Austin was designated as its seat. With no previous mention in any part of Nevada territory, Jones is listed as secretary of Lander Lodge, Free and Accepted Masons, No. 8, at its organization in June 1864.[24] In October he was elected to the County Central Committee by the Democratic County Convention.[25] Apparently this was a stepping stone to his election in November as Deputy Recorder of the county. The next election was held 6 November 1866, but Jones left his position some time before 31 May. Beginning that day, and for a month, he advertised in the newspaper as a "Searcher of Records" and identified himself as the "Ex-Deputy Recorder of Lander County."[26]

---

[23] Entry for 30 July 1858. The clippings are from the "Local and Mining" columns of the local newspaper. "Skillful Penmanship," "An Elaborate Work," "What We Pay, and How We Pay," and "Handsome Emblem," *Daily Reese River* (Austin, Nev.) *Reveille,* 22 March, 3 May, 20 October 1865, 17 March 1866. "Among the Records" and "Penmanship—Masonic Roll of Membership" have not been located.

[24] *Daily Reese River Reveille,* 4 June 1864; [Thomas H. Thompson and Albert A. West], *Reproduction of Thompson and West's History of Nevada. 1881. With Illustrations and Biographical Sketches of Its Prominent Men and Pioneers,* introduction by David F. Myrick (Berkeley, Calif.: Howell-North, 1958), pp. 240–241, 460.

Jones is not listed in two Nevada directories that predate this. J. Wells Kelly, comp., *First Directory of Nevada Territory, Containing the Names of Residents in the Principal Towns; A Historical Sketch, the Organic Act, and Other Political Matters of Interest; Together with a Description of All the Quartz Mills; Reduction Works, and All Other Industrial Establishments in the Territory; as Also of the Leading Mining Claims* (San Francisco: Valentine & Co., 1862); J. Wells Kelly, comp., *Second Directory of Nevada Territory; Embracing a General Directory of Residents of all Principal Towns; Business Directory of Advertisers, Quartz Mills, Reduction Works, Toll Roads, Etc.* (Virginia [City], Nev.: Printed by Valentine & Co., 1863).

[25] *Daily Reese River Reveille,* 19 October 1864.

[26] Ibid., 17 March, 31 May–29 June 1866. Jones had served under E. S.

There are no clues about him beyond this.[27] The remainder of his years is a subject of pure speculation. Without his Fraser goldfields journey journal, Jones would be an even more obscure participant in the frontier restlessness of which he was a part. Contradictorily, given this meticulous account of his overland trek, he may well have kept a journal of his experiences with the Marcy expedition in the early 1850s and accounts of whatever post-overland adventures he may have had. If there were such, if they have survived, and if they are ever discovered, the documentation of the frontier experience will be enriched accordingly.

* * *

The John W. Jones autograph manuscript journal is in the Everett D. Graff Collection of Western Americana, Newberry Library, Chicago, Illinois. Jones made this copy from the original "whose pencilings are nearly obliterated." His comment about the coming of a newspaper to the Red River settlement, referred to above, suggests that Jones may have made the present copy sometime in early 1860 while he was in Portland, Oregon. Except for very few obvious parenthetical additions and some errors of transcription, it seems to be a faithful transcription.[28]

The journal is the basis for the present publication. Jones

Davis, Recorder. "Handsomely Caned," ibid., 1 April 1865; [Thompson and West], *Reproduction of Thompson and West's History of Nevada,* p. 464.

Jones is listed as a registered voter in Austin's Second Ward for 1865–1866. *Daily Reese River Reveille,* 10 April, 12 October 1865, 21 April, 23 October 1866.

[27] Jones is not listed as a resident of Austin or of Lander County in the federal census of 1870. United States Department of Commerce, Bureau of the Census, *Ninth Census of the United States, 1870, Lander County, Nevada* microfilm roll 834, Record Group 29, National Archives, Washington, D.C.

[28] "(Subsequently, we found it to be too true)." Entry for 26 October 1858. "I shall revert to their trials and sufferings hereafter." Entry for 20 December 1858.

It is possible, too, that Jones had inserted these comments on his original manuscript rather than add them as he was making the copy.

included some other items in the notebook. Those that are relevant are noted in context.[29]

Jones furnished two titles for his journal. A mounted label with a decorative manuscript border, on a front endleaf of the manuscript reads:

My Trip
Across the Plains, via: St. Paul
Red River, Saskatchewan River,
Kootonais Pass, Colville,
During 1858 and '59.

The second one appears at the heading of the first journal entry:

My trip from Faribault, Minn., to Oregon, via,
Saskatchewan route, British America—
Account of the country, our
Sufferings and trials, &c.

He uses "Across the Plains" as a running head throughout the manuscript.

The editorial adjustments made in this transcription of the journal are employed solely to clarify reading and understanding of his entries: The text is arbitrarily and logically divided into six chapters. Paragraphing, virtually non-existent in the original, is introduced. The dates for the daily entries are made consistent. The spellings of personal, Indian tribal, and place names are corrected, when possible. The variant orthography of some Indian or Indian-derived words, for example, renders the written form purely arbitrary.

Minor spelling errors, repeated words, flourishes, and other obvious slips of the writer's pen are corrected silently. Periods are added to abbreviations. Ampersands are converted to ands. Ditto marks and "do.s" are expanded to their full form.

[29] For a full physical description of the journal and the other materials in the notebook see Colton Storm, comp., *A Catalogue of the Everett D. Graff Collection of Western Americana* (Chicago: Published for The Newberry Library by University of Chicago Press, 1968), pp. 337–338.

Vagaries or omission of capitalization and punctuation are resolved by choosing, without notice, those that are most appropriate.

The John W. Jones journal is an intimate account of Jones and his traveling companions. The entries carry themselves well. The editorial introductions to each chapter and the notes are designed to give context and explanation for things that may be unfamiliar to the reader, to enhance the story of the expedition. Identification of every person and place, a history of settlements, trading posts, and Indian tribes, and other details are not necessary to understand this journal. Much of this sort of thing has already been included with other journal accounts of Fraser-bound overlanders, particularly those of 1862.[30]

Jones clipped woodcuts from contemporary magazines and pasted them in the notebook. These are used to illustrate his account.

[30] See, for example, Wade, *Overlanders of '62;* McNaughton, *Overland to Cariboo;* and Thomas McMicking, *Overland from Canada to British Columbia. By Mr. Thomas McMicking of Queenston, Canada West,* ed. Joanne Leduc (Vancouver: University of British Columbia Press, 1981).

SURVIVAL ON A WESTWARD TREK

CHAPTER 1

The Journey Begins: Faribault
to Fort Garry

[For purposes of travel, the Faribault party of nine men divided into two messes. This arrangement did not remain intact for the entire trek. The roster expanded and contracted as Jones and his friends traveled towards their objective; and circumstances forced a reassessment and change of their goal.

After a festive sendoff from Faribault, they completed their outfits in St. Paul and headed northward. Travel routes between St. Paul and Fort Garry were well established and in constant use, so the chance of misadventure was minimal.

Jones was a good observer who could write an intimate account of the vicissitudes of travel of the Fraser goldfield-bound Minnesotans. Across Minnesota in a northwesterly direction to the Red River and following that river northward, they moved across the border into Hudson's Bay Company country. While adapting to travel, Jones and his friends were now in another cultural environment. The Fort Garry experience gave them a new perspective and somewhat tempered their chauvinism.]

* * *

TUESDAY, JULY 20, 1858.   On the afternoon of the 20th of July, our little party [was] comprised of the following named persons: J. L. Houck, J. E. Smith, E. Hind, and J. W. Jones—one mess; Wm. Amesbury, I. Emehiser, J. Schaeffter, J.

Palmer, and J. R. Sanford—second mess.[1] Took our departure with regrets and well wishes of the loved ones and friends.[2] In detailing this journal, I confine myself more particularly to the mess to which I belonged. Our journey to Fraser River by the Saskatchewan route was induced by the glowing accounts given of the country, by some one evidently unacquainted with the country, or through mercenary motives, in the *St. Paul [Daily] Pioneer and Democrat,* as also stating as being the shortest route, etc.[3]

---

[1] Jones usually preferred surnames, at times with initials. Sometimes names were expanded: Joseph L. Houck, James Elnathan Smith, Ed C. Hind, Ira Emehiser, John Schaeffter, John Palmer. He occasionally used readily recognizable nicknames as Bill and Joe. Variant spellings and errors in names and initials that occur in newspaper accounts are corrected silently.

[2] For notice of their departure see *Faribault Central Republican,* 20 July, 4 August 1858.

[3] "A meeting of citizens of St. Paul [was] held on Thursday, July 1st, for the purpose of considering the best measures for establishing an emigrant route through the Red River and Saskatchewan Valleys, to the Gold Mines on Fraser and Thompson rivers in British Oregon." A committee was formed and requested to report to another meeting on 7 July. The editor asserted that "The project is feasible [and] *the best route to the Pacific lies through Minnesota and British America." St. Paul Daily Pioneer and Democrat,* 2 July 1858. For a similar report see *Saint Paul Daily Minnesotian,* 2 July 1858; *Saint Paul Weekly Minnesotian,* 3 July 1858.

Three subsequent meetings, 7, 10, 17 July, went into considerable detail about such a route. Further, "reliable testimony" asserted that western Minnesota could be connected to the eastern base of the Rocky Mountains by "continuous steamboat navigation." From here, the goldfields of British Columbia were only eight days journey removed. These meetings were reported in *St. Paul Daily Pioneer and Democrat,* 3, 4, 7, et passim, July 1858; *Saint Paul Daily Minnesotian,* 9, 24 July 1858; *Saint Paul Weekly Minnesotian,* 10 July 1858.

The deliberations were referred by resolution to the state legislature which appointed a select committee on the subject. The committee incorporated the citizens' deliberations and related data in its report to the legislature. Minnesota Legislature, House, Select Committee on Overland Route to British Oregon, *Report.*

This achieved an even wider circulation. The *St. Paul Daily Pioneer and Democrat,* the printer for many state documents, published the legislative

Amesbury's party started in the morning, we started in the afternoon. We only traveled six miles this evening, and camped. Having picketed our horses and mules, we commenced to cook our first meal, our larder having been totally furnished by our friends.

While eating our supper, we were agreeably surprised by a long cavalcade of friends, who had impressed every vehicle that could be found in the town to pay us a flying visit, and witness our camping operations. With admirable forethought, they brought a full supply of liquids, from sparkling champagne to tangle-legged whiskey. Having cleared the ground of our supper, etc., we soon commenced to attack the enemy, nor did we cease till the grey tint of morn appeared in the horizon.

We now bid a last farewell to Messrs. Barron of the Barron House, McCarger & Bro., merchants, [Wm. S.] Judd, banker, Smith & Co., and other well-tried friends. Richard Delprat, banker, and C. Houck, and C[harles] Hind, brothers to two of our party, accompanied us as far as St. Paul.[4]

WEDNESDAY, JULY 21, 1858.   Traveled about thirty-three miles,[5] and camped four miles from Lakeville, on the prairie. During the day, we caught [up] with the ox teams of Amesbury's party. The weather was extremely fine. Nothing worthy of note transpired, but created some surprise with the inhabitants on the road.

THURSDAY, JULY 22, 1858.   Arrived at St. Paul at noon. Distance about twenty miles from last night's camp. Put up

report as a 100-page pamphlet and placed it in local bookstores. On 27 July 1858, and in several successive issues, notice was made of its pending publication. See also advertisement, 29 March 1859. This publication was also noted in *Saint Paul Daily Minnesotian,* 14 August 1858; *Saint Paul Weekly Minnesotian,* 21 August 1858.

[4] The *Faribault Central Republican* carried advertisements for some of these merchants and bankers. See also ibid., 11 August 1858.

[5] Although this distance is confirmed by a numerical notation in the margin, it is an apparent mistake or exaggeration by some ten miles.

St. Paul, Minnesota
From "The Upper Mississippi," Harper's New Monthly Magazine 16
(March 1858)

at the Franklin House, on the suburbs of the city. Spent the remainder of the day in calling upon acquaintances. Weather fine.

FRIDAY, JULY 23, 1858. Occupied in completing our outfit. Bought an additional mule. Daily papers noticed our arrival.[6] Rainy.

SATURDAY, JULY 24, 1858. Morning, occupied myself in writing letters to friends, and a note to Mr. O. Brown, editor and publisher of the *Faribault [Central] Republican*. (No Democratic paper in the town.) Afternoon we left St. Paul and camped two and half miles from St. Anthony.[7] Our two friends

[6] Jones may have referred to the *St. Paul* (Minn.) *Daily Times*. Files for this period are missing, but the *Faribault Central Republican*, 4 August 1858, reprinted a notice of the Jones Party from the *Daily Times*, no date. It noted the arrival "a few days ago" and the planned departure for 26 July.

The *St. Paul Daily Pioneer and Democrat*, 25 July 1858, made general statements about "several companies" and "several parties" preparing to leave or having left St. Paul or other Minnesota locations.

The *Saint Paul Daily Minnesotian*, 24 July 1858, referred to "numerous persons." This newspaper, 26 July 1858, made specific mention of the Jones party, as well as two other parties, and still another planning to leave in the spring. The *Saint Paul Weekly Minnesotian*, 31 July 1858, published the same account. The party that planned to leave Minnesota in the spring decided to depart Minnesota in late summer and to winter at the Selkirk settlement. *Saint Paul Daily Minnesotian*, 20 August 1858; *Saint Paul Weekly Minnesotian*, 21 August 1858. The *Saint Paul Daily Minnesotian*, 5 August 1858, and *Saint Paul Weekly Minnesotian*, 7 August 1858, quoted a traveler who had just come in from the Red River as having met "no less than *seven parties* of emigrants, on their way to New Caledonia [British Columbia]."

[7] The departure from St. Paul was noted by John N. Treadwell, 30 July 1858, in a letter to J. Clark Bush. Gertrude W. Ackerman, ed., "An Optimistic Pioneer in a Period of Depression," *Minnesota History* 13 (June 1932): 174–178.

The party was traveling from St. Paul to St. Cloud on the Metropolitan Trail. Rhoda R. Gilman, Carolyn Gilman, and Deborah M. Stultz, *The Red River Trails: Oxcart Routes Between St. Paul and the Selkirk Settlement, 1820–1870* (St. Paul: Minnesota Historical Society, 1979), pp. 81–87, and accompanying maps.

References are made to specific maps to locate some of the place names

still accompanying us. Weather fine. [Traveled seven and one half miles.][8]

SUNDAY, JULY 25, 1858.   Morning, had a hard thunder storm. Blowed our tent down and got a good wetting in consequence—"the first *wet* of the trip." Bid farewell to Hind, Houck, and Delprat—good fellows. Sorry to part with them. In the evening we were joined by G. Smith and Col. Nobles and some other citizens of St. Paul, who were furnished with an outfit[9] by Col. Nobles and some other citizens of St. Paul.[10]

MONDAY, JULY 26, 1858.   Morning, started early. Passed through St. Anthony, and created no little sensation among its inhabitants when they learned our destination. All wished the pioneer party a safe and prosperous trip. Several young men who were suddenly seized with the gold fever offered their services as cooks, or [to] do any other work that might be required, to take them through, being evidently at the time

and physical geographic features which Jones mentioned in the journal. In addition, topographic maps issued by the United States Geological Survey and by Canada's Department of Energy, Mines, and Resources are helpful for the entire journal. These will be noted for segments of the journey. For Minnesota see United States Geological Survey, Minnesota topographic map 1:500 000.

[8] Jones usually incorporated the day's travel mileage in the text and with a marginal numerical notation. In a few cases it was not indicated at all. If it was omitted in the text and can be supplied from the margin it is put in at the end of that day's entry without further notice.

[9] Including two mules and a cart. *Faribault Central Republican,* 11 August 1858.

[10] Minnesota explorer-politician William H. Nobles had led the Fort Ridgely & South Pass Road construction expedition. G. C. Burnham, who joined the party the next day, Smith, and Charles Goodrich had held "prominent positions" on the expedition.

There is some confusion concerning Smith's name recorded herein as G. Smith. In a letter printed in ibid., 29 September 1858, Jones designated it as W. E. Smith, while the same newspaper on 4 August 1858, gave W. Ellis Smith as the name. The *Saint Paul Daily Minnesotian,* 26 July 1858, and *Saint Paul Weekly Minnesotian,* 31 July 1858, referred to him as Ellis Smith.

destitute of the "shiners." Had to refuse, didn't wish any more to join our mess. In the afternoon, we were joined by G. Burnham of St. Paul who attached himself to the party from the same place.

Camped at night about two miles from Anoka, a small village, containing probably three hundred inhabitants. Bought a large supply of matches at the manufactory. Commencement of our annoyance by the mosquitoes. Character of the country—chiefly timber of stunted growth, openings, sandy soil. Weather fine. Distance, about twenty-five ½ miles.

TUESDAY, JULY 27, 1858.   Passed through the villages of Orono and Elk Town.[11] During the morning, myself and Smith concluded, as we passed a farm, to forage some. Visited a potato patch and procured a good mess. Came very near of being caught. Camped at night opposite Bear Island. Traveled about 30 miles—distance computed by the odometer of Smith of the St. Paul party. Mosquitoes troublesome. Weather rainy and disagreeable. Character of the country unchanged.

WEDNESDAY, JULY 28, 1858.   Today Smith and myself availed ourselves of the last *ardent*. Passed through St. Cloud. Crossed the Mississippi at this place. While in town I wrote to Brown, Tillotson, and Bugbee.[12] Came through some very fine and picturesque country. Traveled about twenty-five miles and camped at St. Josephs, a Jesuitical Mission.[13] Weather

[11] Orono has since been absorbed by the village of Elk River. This Orono is not the present western Minneapolis suburb of the same name. Gilman, Gilman, and Stultz, *Red River Trails,* p. 82.

[12] Correspondents Bugbee and Tillotson were mentioned again by Jones on 14 August, but they were not further identified.

[13] St. Joseph was a German settlement.

Beyond St. Cloud, Jones and his party were on the Old Middle Trail which they followed north and westward to the Red River above Breckenridge. Also known as the St. Cloud, Sauk River, Sauk Rapids, Plains, and East Plains Trail, it followed the divide between the watersheds of the Minnesota and the upper Mississippi rivers. Gilman, Gilman, and Stultz, *Red River Trails,* pp. 69–80, and accompanying maps.

rainy. Crossed Sauk River on a bridge. During the night our frying pan was stolen by some thieving and heartless Dutch-man, a resident of St. Josephs.

THURSDAY, JULY 29, 1858.   Crossed Sauk River again at Richmond. This station is also a Jesuitical Mission.[14] The country around is beautiful, being prairie and timber equally diversified. Procured a handleless frying pan from a resident, Hon. *Somebody,* on the opposite [side of] the river. Crossed the river on a ferry. Camped on Richmond prairie. Soil rich. Weather fine. Traveled twenty-four miles.

FRIDAY, JULY 30, 1858.   This morning while riding, I lost my splendid meerschaum, a gift of Bro. H. D. Bristol, lawyer, a man endeared to me not only by association as a foster brother, but by more and worthy motives—that of the "mystic tie." I regretted the loss very much and spent two or three hours in vain search for it. Crossed several sloughs and got mired several times. Rained hard all day.

At noon, we overtook a Red River train homeward bound. They were camped near a lake waiting for reinforcements, as they were afraid of the predatory bands of Sioux who infested that portion of the country and who would not spare a train that came in their way if numerically stronger.[15] The train was composed of half-breeds, with Red River carts, a curiosity by the way, being destitute of iron with the exception of the staples in the shafts. They work mostly oxen. From them we procured a little of "Red Eye" which proved salutary in its effects, considering the condition we were then in, having been wet from early dawn and with no prospects of drying soon. Bidding them good-by, we passed lakes Henry and George. Rained hard all day. Country prairie and timber. Soil rich.

---

[14] Richmond was a German settlement. Ibid., p. 79.

"Richmond is another Catholic Mission, it boasts of two houses, both of which are stores." *Faribault Central Republican,* 29 September 1858.

[15] The "rumored . . . band" of 400 Sioux warriors awaited them at Long Prairie. *Faribault Central Republican,* 29 September 1858.

Night very chilly and mosquitoes troublesome. Traveled sixteen miles.

SATURDAY, JULY 31, 1858.   Our traveling this morning was very bad. Mired three times. Afternoon the traveling was very good. Weather clear and fine. Character of the country chiefly prairie, but considerable timber. Soil second rate. Traveled twenty-one miles. Crossed [North Fork] Crow River. Not very deep, waded. Camped at Twin Lakes.

Between the two lakes a solitary log cabin stood, inhabited by a solitary old bachelor, who, disgusted with the world, had settled there to be clear of the din and strife of civilization.[16] Twin Lakes is a romantic looking spot and very appropriately named as there is but a very narrow strip of land that divides the two lakes. The country around is beautiful. After supper, I took a ride with the old bach in a canoe. During the excursion I noticed some very fine bass and pike, but not having a hook and line I could not entice the finny tribe on board. On this lake I noticed a yellow pond flower that I never witnessed before, but they were not attractive. Camped at the cabin. Weather clear.

SUNDAY, AUGUST 1, 1858.   Bid farewell to our bachelor host. At noon we passed White Bear Lake.[17] The scenery around this lake, which is large, surpassed anything in picturesque beauty, anything I had yet seen. It was truly all that an artist desired. The soil, however, where we traversed is gravelly and rocky. At this place we caught up with the ox teams of Amesbury's party, and from this place we traveled together. They had left us at St. Paul. They made no stoppage. Met a party of surveyors who had been out on government surveys, but now were homeward bound. Traveling in the morning

[16] "There is a town site laid out at this place, which boasts of one log house and a foundation for another." Ibid.

The two lakes are probably McCloud Lake and Grove Lake. Gilman, Gilman, and Stultz, *Red River Trails,* pp. 74–76.

[17] White Bear Lake is now Lake Minnewaska. Gilman, Gilman, and Stultz, *Red River Trails,* p. 76.

very good, afternoon vice versa. Wood and water plenty. Character of the country generally good 1st rate soil. Traveled thirty miles. Rain in the afternoon.

MONDAY, AUGUST 2, 1858.   Crossed Rapid[18] and Pomme de Terre Rivers. Crossing Rapid River was very bad, but Pomme de Terre was good. Passed several small lakes. Two very beautiful lakes that we passed we named lakes Charlotte and Mary, after two *dear ones* we left behind us. But I doubt very much whether the names will be perpetuated. Saw fresh Indian signs, in the shape of moccasin tracks. Traveling fair. Trail still plain. Traveled thirty-four miles. Character of the country unchanged. Camped at Lake Delprat, named by us after a warm hearted friend. Rained hard all night, and the mosquitoes finding a good shelter from the rain proved very annoying.

TUESDAY, AUGUST 3, 1858.   Passed Lightning Lake, a very beautiful and shallow lake. Today timber was very scarce. The Traveling was bad, owing to the heavy rains. During the day we had one of our wagons break down, but soon repaired the damage. Water plenty. Arrived at Otter Tail River in the evening and camped on the opposite banks. The river is about eighty feet wide with a very bad and miry bottom. Depth of ford about three feet. Had another shower in the afternoon. We are now getting used to being wet. Mosquitoes very troublesome at night. Traveled 21½ miles.

WEDNESDAY, AUGUST 4, 1858.   For the first five miles this morning we traveled through very low and swampy ground, consequently the traveling was bad; the rest of our march through was very good. Having ascended the headlands we found a dry and hard road. I noticed several spots today on the prairie thickly covered with small shells, a convincing proof that at one time it had been a large lake. At one o'clock P.M. the thermometer stood at 100 degrees. Weather very hot and sultry. Arrived at Red River crossing, just below Graham's

---

[18] Rapid River is probably Chippewa River. Ibid., pp. 73, 76.

Point, about three o'clock. At this river we came across a man who came from Breckenridge in a bateau, going to Graham's Point. Bought his bateau for thirty dollars. Loaded it to relieve our animals, and started it for Pembina in charge of Messrs. J. E. Smith, J. R. Sanford, G. Smith, and Burnham.[19] Crossed the river at eve and camped on its banks.[20]

Having now come to the heart of the Indian country, we concluded to set night watches, first watch from dark till 12 m[idnight], the second from 12 m. to daylight. About midnight we were aroused from our slumbers by an alarm of the guard. Upon coming to our senses he showed us the object of his fears, which was a campfire at Graham's Point. Things looked squally. We had recourse to the *armory*[21] and stood for some minutes in fearful expectation of a sudden onslaught by the thieving red dogs. At last one of our party made the remark that he thought it was the campfire of the man from whom we bought the bateau, and all joined in the same opinion, but as our fears were not totally dispelled we slept but very little the remainder of the night. Wood and water scarce to the river. Traveled twenty-four miles. Soil 1st, 2d, and third rate.

THURSDAY, AUGUST 5, 1858.   For the first sixteen miles we saw no water. There is no stream on the trail between the crossing of Red and Wild Rice rivers. As the day was exces-

[19] They loaded the boat with 2500 pounds of freight. *Toronto Globe,* 7 October 1858.

[20] The party here crossed the Red River into present North Dakota to move northward on the River Trail which they hoped to follow to the Red River settlement. Gilman, Gilman, and Stultz, *Red River Trails,* pp. 27–33, 36–37, 41–42, and accompanying maps. See also United States Geological Survey, North Dakota topographic map 1:500 000.

They did get lost and wandered some on the way to Pembina, but Jones does not give sufficient information to follow the wanderings. See his entries for 7, 8 August below.

[21] This is a reference to Fort Abercrombie, a mile or so down river from Graham's Point. These points are a short distance down the Red River from present Breckenridge, Minnesota. Gilman, Gilman, and Stultz, *Red River Trails,* pp. 37, 41.

sively hot both men and animals suffered from want of water. Wild Rice River is bridged, the work of Red River Half-breeds. This river is skirted by a small belt of timber. Came to Cheyenne [Sheyenne] River about five o'clock in the evening. This river we also found bridged and is also skirted by a small strip of timber.

During my travels throughout the different sections of the States, and especially in the swamps of Louisiana and other southern states, I harbored the idea that I had seen a *few* mosquitoes, but there is no comparison between the two. The air was perfectly darkened with them. Our poor animals were perfectly frantic, and in spite of the continual switching with a brush they still clung to us with annoying tenacity for several miles; and in fact we traveled till about eleven at night in order to get away from the mosquito empire. Our animals feeling the effects of hard driving, we concluded to stop and cut up our tents and cover them with it. Camped on the prairie. Grass very tall. Built smudges with dry grass. The animals laid down, and in a measure relieved themselves of the pestilence as we found that the mosquitoes did not come very low down. I never in the whole course of my life saw any species of insects that were so bloodthirsty as these rapacious devils were. Traveled thirty-five miles. Wood and water very scarce. Soil rich.

FRIDAY, AUGUST 6, 1858.   Had a stampede this morning and had hard work to regain some of our loose animals; but thanks to Amesbury's company who had camped about two miles below us, had it not been for them we would have lost them. At noon we came to a small stream and concluded to camp there and rest our animals. Rained hard all morning. Wood and water plenty. Weather cold and cloudy. Traveled sixteen miles and a half. Mosquitoes not as troublesome but still plenty.

SATURDAY, AUGUST 7, 1858.   During our morning's travel the trail became so indistinct that eventually we [were] lost.

Sent a horseman across the country to look for it. Cut across ourselves in an oblique line from our scout. After two or three hours travel we again struck it. Crossed no running streams today. Our road was principally through sloughs and were bad. No timber. Had to use "buffalo chips" to cook our evening meal. Soil over track we passed from third to first rate. Camped on Buffalo Creek. Weather cool and pleasant. Traveled 23½ miles.

SUNDAY, AUGUST 8, 1858.   Thinking that we were on the wrong trail, we again cut across the country and soon had the pleasure of finding a well beat trail which we followed. Killed two prairie chickens which proved a savory mess. Character of the country, rolling prairie intersected with marshes; soil first rate. Crossed two small streams, names unknown to me. Morning was quite foggy. Witnessed as soon as the fog cleared a splendid mirage which came near leading us astray. Traveled twenty-eight and a half miles.

MONDAY, AUGUST 9, 1858.   Soon after we started this morning one of our party happening to look ahead saw a black object what he thought at first a small clump of bushes, but on watching he saw it move. Soon it became apparent it must be a buffalo. Houck and Hind immediately took their guns, mounted their horses, and gave pursuit. The chase was exciting. Houck upon coming within range of his unerring rifle dismounted and fired; and as he fired his horse left him, frightened. The bull was seen to stagger; and at this moment Hind came up and let him have the contents of both barrels in a ticklish part, which brought him to the ground. We soon dispatched him and replenished our larder with the most choice portions, leaving the rest to the wolves and vultures. We saw no more buffalo that day. We afterwards learned that the Red River train which preceded us killed a drove of seventy buffaloes at this place, and he was evidently the only one that escaped.

Road today chiefly through sloughs. Mosquitoes inclined to

be troublesome. No wood in sight, had to cook our meals with the ever-ready "buffalo chips." Crossed two small running streams, names unknown. Water plenty. Weather fair. Traveled 19½ miles.

TUESDAY, AUGUST 10, 1858.   The traveling this morning was good, but in the afternoon it was a succession of swamps. Crossed five small running streams. No timber yet in sight. Weather moderate. Troubled during the day very much with mosquitoes, horseflies, and buffalo gnats. Character of the country unchanged. Traveled 27 miles.

WEDNESDAY, AUGUST 11, 1858.   Crossed a strip of low land thickly covered with blue joint grass, very tall. The strip was about fourteen miles in length. Had considerable difficulty in extricating ourselves from a slough. Picked chokecherries today. Crossed three small running streams. Weather warm and cloudy. Character of the country changing for the better with rich soil. Camped near timber.

During the night John Schaeffter, better known as Dutch John, while on watch was indiscreet enough to set fire to the prairie to drive off the mosquitoes. It was with great deal of difficulty that we could put it out, as a portion of the Company had to look to the animals as they had taken fright and were on the eve of a stampede. Wood and water plenty. Traveled twenty-eight miles.

THURSDAY, AUGUST 12, 1858.   The traveling throughout the morning was excellent, but in the afternoon it was villainous. Crossed a marsh seven miles in width with the water nearly up to the wagon beds nearly the whole distance.[22] Charley Goodrich succeeded in killing some ducks. Weather changeable. Camped on the prairie. Timber scarce again. Traveled twenty-seven miles.

---

[22] They called it the Slough of Despond. *Faribault Central Republican*, 29 September 1858.

FRIDAY, AUGUST 13, 1858.   Arrived at Pembina about 11 o'clock, A.M. Trail this morning very bad. Crossed Pembina River on a ferry. We were kindly welcomed into the village by Jas. McFetridge Esq., U.S. Port Collector. Pembina is situated at the confluence of Pembina and Red River. It contains three adobe houses and half a dozen log shanties.[23] The inhabitants are half-breeds; but two white men live there, Hon. Joe Rolette, State Senator for the Pembina District and Jas. McFetridge. Mr. Rolette was not at home. We left him at St. Paul. We had cultivated the acquaintance of McF. in St. Paul prior to our departure. Through his kindness we found a good camping ground in the vicinity of the village. The inhabitants, both Indians and half-breeds, subsist almost entirely upon fish and game. I had forgot to state that Pembina was only a mile and a half from the United States boundary line.[24]

We saw today quite a number of Chippewa Indians. They were very friendly. The country around is very low and is subject almost yearly to the overflow of Red River. The soil is rich but is very little cultivated. From last night's camp to Pembina was 13½ miles. Weather cool and pleasant.

SATURDAY, AUGUST 14, 1858.   Stayed in camp. Bateau has not arrived. Wrote to Brown, Tillotson, Bugbee, and Delprat. Weather fine. Mosquitoes plenty. Ed Hind went to Fort Garry this morning to see his cousin, in company with Mr. McF. Nothing worthy of note transpired. Indians visiting us, and we visiting the Indians in return.

SUNDAY, AUGUST 15, 1858.   G. Smith of the bateau party came in this morning barefooted and in a pitiable plight,

---

[23] Except for the roof, they closely resembled Central American houses, "but on a closer examination we found them to be built of hewn logs, plastered both inside and out with clay. The roofs are thatched with straw and bark. They have the appearance of being warm and comfortable." Ibid.

[24] An odometer calculation registered 521 miles from Faribault to Pembina "by the outside trail." They received assurances from "reliable sources" that the distance was one hundred miles shorter by "the Crow Wing route." Ibid.

PEMBINA, AND MOUTH OF PEMBINA RIVER.

Pembina, and Mouth of Pembina River
From Manton Marble, "To Red River and Beyond," Harper's New
Monthly Magazine 21 (October 1860)

having been three [days] and nights without food. It appears that he got out of the boat at a point on the river and [decided to] walk for a recreation to the next point. Having arrived there, he waited some time for the bateau to come along. Finally tired of waiting and entertaining the idea that it had passed, he trudged along and finally lost himself. Having started with nothing on his feet but a pair of moccasins, he soon wore them out in the grass. Finding no trail, he concluded that it would be best for him to follow the banks of the river, which he did. He was a miserable looking specimen of the *genus homo* when he made his *entre* into our camp. His feet were badly lacerated. We soon had him a meal cooked for him by Mrs. Rolette, and the way he made the viands disappear was truly astonishing to the natives. He never strayed away from the party after that. Visited the British fort.[25]

MONDAY, AUGUST 16, 1858.   Bateau arrived early this morning.[26] They cursed like devils at the tediousness of the voyage and the crookedness of the river. Traded one of our American horses for an Indian pony and cart. Again visited the fort which is situated on the banks of the river nearly on the line. The fort is built of logs, the hewed pickets outside set up endways. Around the fort we saw a number of Indian lodges. Some of the Indian braves were disposed to be rather impudent; but, on a sight of a cudgel we had in our hands, they wisely forbore. They probably thought that we had come to procure some rum, which in truth was our errand; but we failed to get any; and [they] intended to frighten us in order to capture it. I killed five prairie

---

[25] This was a Hudson's Bay Company trading post located less than a half mile north of the boundary line. William E. Lass, *Minnesota's Boundary with Canada: Its Evolution since 1783* (St. Paul: Minnesota Historical Society Press, 1980), p. 74; Gilman, Gilman, and Stultz, *Red River Trails*, p. 33.

There is no trading post journal for this date in the Hudson's Bay Company Archives, Provincial Archives of Manitoba. Judith Hudson Beattie to author, August 19, 1987.

[26] This detail and information about the party's progress and plans were reported in the *Toronto Globe,* 7 October 1858.

PEMBINA FORT.

Pembina Fort
From Manton Marble, "To Red River and Beyond," Harper's New
Monthly Magazine 21 (October 1860)

chickens near camp. Weather rainy. Loaded our carts and wagons. Mosquitoes plenty and troublesome.

TUESDAY, AUGUST 17, 1858.   Left Pembina.[27] Crossed Kankakee, which was bad. Crossed Scratching River[28] on a ferry. Met an Indian with a team going to Fort Garry. Weather fine. Trail plain but in bad condition. Wood and water plenty. Country low and marshy, prairie interspersed with poplar of small growth. Camped at Scratching River. Mosquitoes troublesome. Traveled 26 miles. The St. Paul party, Messrs. Goodrich, Smith, and Burnham, not being able to complete their outfit are awaiting the arrival of Mr. Rolette, who promised to assist them.[29]

WEDNESDAY, AUGUST 18, 1858.   Entered Selkirk settlement[30] in the afternoon. Roads very bad. Character of the country unchanged. Weather fine. Wood and water plenty. Rained hard all night. Traveled 27 miles.

THURSDAY, AUGUST 19, 1858.   Crossed Stinking River.[31] Character of the country unchanged. Roads very bad. Met McFetridge on his way home. Induced him to return.

[27] From Pembina northward, the Red River Trail was sometimes called the Pembina Trail. Gilman, Gilman, and Stultz, *Red River Trails*, p. 31, and accompanying map. See also Canada, Department of Energy, Mines, and Resources, Brandon-Winnipeg [Manitoba] topographic map 1:500 000.

[28] What Jones called the Kankakee was probably the Riviere aux Marais or Marsh River which was described as "a treacherous morass." Scratching River is Morris River on modern maps. Gilman, Gilman, and Stultz, *Red River Trails*, pp. 31–33.

[29] Burnham, Goodrich, and Smith resumed their journey later. They spent the winter and worked at Fort Pitt or Fort Edmonton, probably the latter. Departing there on 19 May 1859, they reached The Dalles, 31 August. *St. Paul Daily Pioneer and Democrat,* 3 August 1859; a notice, probably from *The Dalles Journal,* undated, copied by Jones at the end of his journal, briefly describes the leg of the Goodrich party journey.

[30] Thomas Douglas, Earl of Selkirk, had established a colony on the Red River on a grant of land from the Hudson's Bay Company. Arthur S. Morton, *History of the Canadian West,* pp. 537–540.

[31] Stinking River is Riviere Sale. Gilman, Gilman, and Stultz, *Red River Trails,* pp. 31, 32.

During our morning's march a laughable incident took place in which Jim Smith was the party concerned. Jim and myself had lagged behind with our respective teams. Coming to a slough, Jim's team passed over in safety. He had taken his breeches off to mend them as he was riding along. I was following close in his wake, but the moment I got into the slough the obstinate and obstreperous beast could not be induced to move or budge either by coaxing or castigation. I requested Jim to stop and help me. We unfastened the Indian perverseness from the shafts; got him on dry ground; fastened ropes to the shafts and hitched him to it, who soon brought it out. As soon as we were out Jim started for his team; and it had just started on a run, Jim after him with the tail of his shirt fluttering in the breeze.

Such a picture. It was so ludicrous that I came near collapsing. I immediately put the gad to old obstinacy after the flying team and the maniac Jim. We kept up the gait for nearly half a mile; and turning a sharp angle of the road, we perceived that a person had stopped the runaway and was returning with him. Jim was frantic at the dilemma in which he was caught, and donning his off cast garment he vented his wrath on the poor beast in such a manner that he soon got tired. I think, however, that it taught the horse a lesson, for he was never known to run away after; but on the contrary it was repeatedly known that he wouldn't pull when in a bad place unless he was hitched by the tail.

Fort Garry is situated at the junction of the Assinniboine and Red Rivers and holds a commanding position.[32] The barracks is surrounded with a stone wall, with towers mounted with guns of small caliber at each corner. It was occupied by two companies of the Canadian Royal Rifles, and the Hudson's Bay Company's attaches.

---

[32] Fort Garry should not be confused with the still standing Lower Fort Garry, erected in the 1830s twenty miles down river at Selkirk, Manitoba. Ibid., pp. 28–30.

Fort Garry
From Manton Marble, "To Red River and Beyond," Harper's New Monthly Magazine 22 (February 1861)

Mr. Mactavish, the chief Factor of the District and master of the fort,[33] upon learning of our arrival, came to us to extend his hospitality and invite us to take quarters at the fort, during our stay there. Upon meeting us, he inquired of one of our company who was the *gentleman* of the party, entertaining I have no doubt of English customs and the idea that there was but one gentleman and the rest were servants. Hind informed him that we were all gentlemen. It proved too obtuse for him. He then inquired how many servants we had with us; and the reply was that we had no servants, that everyone had to serve for himself. This also proved to be rather curious to him, as he remarked that when *we* travel *we* are always accompanied by servants. We told him that such a thing was not known in the United States.

He informed us that he had prepared quarters for us at the garrison and would be pleased to see us occupy them. We thanked him for his generous offer and politely declined, preferring to camp out. Furthermore that some of our party might during our stay be a little influenced by the ardent and create a rumpus in the garrison while in that state, especially so if a discussion took place upon the respective merits of the two nations; and as we were under obligations for his kind offer, we could not think of accepting and run the risk of paying his hospitality by any breach of hospitality. Upon declining, he invited us to the fort to take a drink, which we accepted; and he gave us about a half gallon of rum to take with us to the camp. Among the soldiers we noticed three or four veterans wearing the Victoria medal upon their left breast for their gallant conduct in the Crimean War.

The Hudson's Bay Stores, warehouses, Chief Factor's residence, officers and privates' quarters, magazines, and everything pertaining thereto are all enclosed with this fortification.

---

[33] William Mactavish was also the governor of the Red River colony, sometimes called Assiniboia. W. Stewart Wallace, *The Dictionary of Canadian Biography,* 2d ed., 2 vols. (Toronto: Macmillan Co., 1945), 2:433; *Dictionary of Canadian Biography,* s.v. "McTavish, William," by N. Jaye Goossen.

On the inside and near the top of the wall are placed sentry walks. The parade ground is very small, not being room enough for the two companies to make their evolutions with ease. I should judge that these poor soldiers fare pretty hard as they complained considerably to us. We saw two or three groups outside of the fort cooking their dinner; and on examining the "flesh pots," we could observe nothing but fresh water herrings, or hickory shads as some term them; but there they are known as "silver sides" and "gold eyes." They are small, very bony, and contain but little meat.

The captain commanding introduced himself to us. His name has slipped my memory. During our conversation, and the topic of the conversation was the British and American armies, during which he uttered the *treasonable* wish that if he held the same position in the American army he would be perfectly satisfied and contented with his lot. He entertained a good opinion of the regulations, the system of appointments and gradation, as well as salaries of American officers in the military service. He also intimated that if he ever was so fortunate as to get an appointment through any influence which might be brought forth, that he would immediately upon the receipt of the news throw up his commission and enter the service of the United States. We informed him that if he retired from the British army and take up his residence in some portion of the thickly populated eastern states and cultivate the acquaintance of some of our great political *guns* who had unbounded influence at the White House, that he might eventually succeed, especially a man of his address and who had seen so much of military service.

Surrounding the fort is quite a town on both sides of the Assinniboine and Red River[34] containing some three or four stores or trading houses, some of whom are Americans, among

---

[34] Soon to be known as Winnipeg. Arthur S. Morton, *History of the Canadian West,* pp. 853–854.

whom we would particularly mention Messrs. Cavalier and Sergeant, two resident partners of the American Fur Trading Company whose headquarters are at St. Paul, Minnesota, and to whom we are indebted for many acts of kindness during our stay there. I should judge that the number of inhabitants on both sides of the rivers is nearly if not quite a thousand. Blacksmiths and carpenters are scarce; and the few that were there grumbled at the extremely low wages they were receiving and also of being in Hudson's Bay shinplasters, specie being very scarce.

The town can also boast of a good gunsmith; and to which I can bear testimony, for I gave him a job of putting a new spring to a Colt's Bull-dog, which he done in a very neat and satisfactory manner and charged very reasonably. Apropos to the occasion,while conversing with this gunsmith, who is a native of Scotland but has been for many years in British America so long that he has almost forgotten everything connected with the old country, after questioning me as to my nativity, avocations, etc., and receiving satisfactory answers, he commenced to give a flattering account of the country and what splendid inducements there were here for some enterprising Americans. He said that he liked Americans, as they were spunky and would not be domineered over by the Hudson's Bay Company nor any other body of men, but were ever ready to maintain at the risk of their own lives their own independence; and for this he admired them, and hoped to see the day when that portion of the country would be under the jurisdiction of the U.S. government. He had long been under the employment of the Hudson's Bay Company, and consequently was well informed of their tyrannical actions to their employees.

As a further inducement for me to stop, he informed me that I might have his daughter for a partner, pointing to her as she entered to call him to supper. Curious to gaze upon the *offering*, I naturally turned to gaze upon her. She was I judge about sixteen, dark, quadroon-quarter Indian, medium height and somewhat pretty. She was the very personification of retired simplicity, gay but modest. No intellectual refinement could be discerned. Hearing her father's words and his question if she would not consent, I noticed a perceptible blush; and at the same time she gave an evasive answer. The old man did not like it. He demanded a peremptory answer; but she was equally as resolute, and the only answer he received was a quick and silent retreat from the shop, much to my relief. Having settled with the old man for his work, I took my departure with the promise that I would call again, and one that I never fulfilled.

The settlements of Selkirk extend for the length of about eighty miles on Red River and about forty miles on the Assinniboine. The inhabitants consist principally of French, Scotch, Canadians, and North Englishmen. But by far the larger portion are half-breeds, and quarter-bloods. They cultivate but little; and the largest farm in the settlements cannot boast over twenty acres, as they are by treaty only allowed by the Indians but a very narrow strip on each side of the river. Wheat, oats, and barley is about the only thing they cultivate; but very [many] vegetables are raised. Their principal diet is pemmican and flour and such fresh game as may by chance fall in their way. Many of the settlers during the summer pay a visit and camp out at Lake Winnipeg, distant forty miles from Ft. Garry, when they procure an abundance of water game, ducks, geese, etc.

The settlement has several churches of different denominations, but principally Catholic and Episcopalian. They have a very large and fine cathedral on the opposite side of the river from Fort Garry, being the seat of the bishopric of the District.[35] The buildings are all with but few exceptions old fashioned and quaintly built. The population of the whole settlement is estimated at 8,000. At this time they had no press; but now as I am copying my old journal whose pencilings are

[35] The St. Boniface Cathedral. Ibid., p. 804.

nearly obliterated, I have been informed that the light of the "Press" has dawned upon them. Success attend it; for it was much needed in that benighted region. Many of its citizens have never seen an apple or any other ripe fruit with which our western states in their seasons are wont to luxuriate. The country is low and flat, interspersed with small growth of cottonwood and balm of Gilead. The land at this point has been known to have flooded twice since the commencement of the settlement; and the inhabitants had to remove their goods and chattels some distance. Trains of hunters are continually coming from and going to the buffalo country.

Pemmican is made from buffalo meat. The process of making it is as I am informed as follows: The lean is divided from the fat when fresh. They then dig a large hole in the ground, covered [sic] it such manner with stones, keep a slow fire all the time. The lean meat is then placed upon these stones. As the meat is dried they take it off and pound it very fine. They then fill a bag made of buffalo hide and fill it full; and then pour in the hot fat which is boiled in kettles, so that when cool there is nearly as much fat as lean. The bag is then sown with sinews. This article of food although not palatable at the beginning surpasses any other as a nourishment to the hunter and traveler in the cold regions of the North.

Weather fine. Soil rich. Wood and water plenty. Traveled twelve miles.

FRIDAY, AUGUST 20, 1858.   Occupied nearly all day in making our final outfit. Traded off all of our American horses and wagons, for oxen, Indian horses, and Red River carts. Also laid in 200 pounds of pemmican. Bought a tea kettle at the fort for which we had to [pay] £210d., which we considered rather steep; but as we could not very well do with[out] it, we paid him without grumbling. Also bought frying pans and other cooking utensils, clothing, etc. The clothing we found to be cheap, even more so than in the States.

We were called upon by a number of the natives and residents of the town; and from them we gleaned considerable information of the country we would pass through. They have no conception of miles. They measure by the day; or if it is less than a day it is then so many "smokes" from point to point. From this we would judge that they have stated times for smoking. They made a great hubbub at the fort today, fired their guns, played "God Save the Queen" just because the Governor of Prince Rupert's Land was going to leave for Canada.[36] We had a glimpse of the governor. He was a very good specimen of the "beef-eating" and "port-loving" John Bull. Looked as though he might make a good alderman for some ward in a large city, if obesity is the qualification necessary to fill such a position. The governor, too deeply immersed with the affairs of the nation, did not deign to notice the arrival of the "blasted Yankees." He was escorted out of the town by the soldiery.

We again visited the fort and were politely shown all around the establishment by the orderly sergeant, detailed for that purpose by the captain commandant. After our curiosity had been gratified and it being near dinner time, we were pressed by several of the privates to dine with them, which we politely refused. Received an invitation to sup with Mr. Sergeant at the residence of his partner Mr. C. Cavalier, who was absent, which we accepted. After sundown we crossed the river in a canoe, and the charge was only a penny and half penny apiece. This we thought was confoundedly cheap as the river is considerably wide; you won't catch an American doing that much work for so little, "not much." They know the *price of labor* too well for that.

Arriving at the house we were introduced to Mrs. Cavalier and had a very social time. Mrs. C. retired after some time had elapsed and left the field clear; and receiving an assurance

[36] Sir George Simpson was governor of Rupert's Land, the Hudson's Bay Company territory. Arthur S. Morton, *Sir George Simpson, Overseas Governor of the Hudson's Bay Company: A Pen Picture of a Man of Action* ([Portland, Oreg.]: Published by Binsford-Mart for the Oregon Historical Society, 1944), frontispiece; p. 278. For a more complete and recent study see John S. Galbraith, *The Little Emperor: Governor Simpson of the Hudson's Bay Company* (Toronto: Macmillan of Canada, 1976).

that no petticoat would intrude upon us we commenced to "work" in earnest; nor did we cease till we became *oblivious* and *tired*. There was no beds required that night; the floor was plenty good enough. During the fore part of our merriness, a pistol report was heard; and Mr. Sergeant remarked that he would bet a gallon of the best "redeye" that could be procured that one of our party fired the shot. Being of the same opinion, we did not accept his offer.

Amesbury's party also traded their American oxen for Red River stock and carts, as well as laying in a supply of pemmican. One of this party, John Palmer, having a difficulty with his mess, separated from them and attached himself to our company on condition that he should cook and wash for us throughout the voyage. He was a queer specimen of humanity. A native of England, he had long served as jockey at races, footman and servant in general to some corpulent and gouty beefeater. *According to his account*, he had been on every inhabitable spot of the globe, perfectly acquainted with the customs and habits of every nation and every clime. No science was too obtuse for him. He knew the nature of every manner of fowl, beasts, fish, reptiles, and insects—perfectly conversant with botany, geology, astronomy, metaphysics, etc. In fact, what he didn't know wasn't worth knowing; and yet this learned savant was almost totally ignorant of the primary department of English education.[37]

[37] The terse entries in the Fort Garry post journal made no mention or inference of the presence of the Jones party. Hudson's Bay Company Archives, Provincial Archives of Manitoba, Winnipeg Post Journal, 1858–1860, B.235/a/16, microfilm, reel 1M154.

CHAPTER 2

Plunging into the Wilderness:
Fort Garry to Fort Carlton

[The Fraser-bound gold seekers now headed westward from Fort Garry. They had traded their horse-drawn wagons and were now traveling with ox-drawn Red River carts. The settlement dwindled rapidly and soon they were in the wilderness, the domain of an occasional trader or band of Indians.

Jones refers to some of the people he encounters as half-breeds. This is one of several terms such as mixed bloods and metis that are used to designate persons of mixed Indian-European parentage or descent living in the prairies of western Canada. Marcel Giraud's classic study of these people has recently been translated and republished.

Aside from lakes, rivers, and other physical landmarks, the party's points of reference for travel consisted mainly of the trading posts of Hudson's Bay Company, variously known as forts or houses, such as Fort Edmonton or Edmonton House. These were usually located at trail junctures, on rivers, or at other strategic places. Fur brigades and traders traveled between these posts along the by-now-familiar routes.

The Carlton Trail was a chain of HBC posts from Fort Garry to Fort Edmonton, sometimes easily recognized from heavy usage but not always, and sometimes with local variations or branches. The Jones party was following this trail across the prairie lands to the Rocky Mountains. It took about a month to reach Fort Carlton, somewhat over half way. Life on the

trail became less uncertain when they encountered and decided to travel with a free trader and his small party also
following the trail for quite some distance.]

*   *   *

SATURDAY, AUGUST 21, 1858.   Morning occupied in loading
our carts, etc. Called upon the officers of the fort. Bid farewell.
Chief Factor Mactavish very kindly offered us letters of introduction as well as orders to the several forts on our route to
supply us with provisions. Deeming it not necessary, as we
had provisions enough to last us six months with the game we
might kill on the road, the offered was thankfully declined by
our commandant Hind for reasons best known to himself. It
surely was an oversight, for the letters would have done us
much good provided we should come in need. We heard today
that two men from Mankato, Minnesota, had started a week
ago from that place destined for the same country.

Bidding farewell to Mr. Sergeant and Mr. McFetridge, we
pulled up stakes and started. On our way, Amesbury and
myself being somewhat influenced by the rosy loitered in the
rear. After trudging along about three miles and a half, we
met a couple of blooming half-breed damsels searching for
cows. Pretending to have lost the track of our company, we
enquired for the nearest house. The eldest spying the absent
cattle, remarked that if we would help to drive them up, they
would take us there, which was their home. Oh, charming
rural simplicity. My mind was now confused and chaotic, continually wandering from the Eldorado we had in view to the
dusky hue of our fair guides. Amesbury enjoyed himself
immensely.

Soon we arrived at the house; and the worthy host invited
us to sup with them as supper was ready, which we gladly
accepted, not because we wanted to refresh the inner man but
still linger as long as possible to our charming cicerones. Our
supper consisted of broiled venison steaks, graham bread and
milk—good enough for anybody and greatly relished by us.

After supper, our host anticipating our wishes brought forth the *jug;* and we sat down to enjoy ourselves till rather late. We intimated our desire to be shown to the residence of Mr. John Roan, as our party were to camp there. He invited us to stay all night; but fearing that our company would be uneasy about our absence we declined his kind offer. Bidding farewell to our fair companions we sallied out, guided by our host, and soon reached camp.

I forgot to mention that the firing last night was done by our night watch at camp. One of those thieving Indian dogs who are always hungry had come too close to our bacon; and as he had continually clubbed them away till forbearance had ceased to be a virtue, he fired. An uproar, and a yell from the canine was the consequence. The sentinels at the fort also raised the alarm, it being extremely uncommon to hear a shot at midnight. Distance from Ft. Garry 4 miles.[1]

---

[1] At times going astray, the party followed the nine hundred mile Carlton Trail from Fort Garry to Fort Edmonton. It went up the Assiniboine River from present Winnipeg to Fort Ellice near the mouth of the Qu'Appelle River near present St. Lazare in western Manitoba. Striking overland, it traversed the wilderness in a northwesterly direction to Fort Carlton on the North Saskatchewan River some fifty miles due north of present Saskatoon, Saskatchewan. From there it moved overland generally northwestward and approximating the direction of the North Saskatchewan River, by way of Fort Pitt on the North Saskatchewan River not far from the western Saskatchewan border above Lloydminster. Again, westerly, the trail went overland to Fort Edmonton, also on the river. There were occasional branches or variations of the trail. The history of the trail is set forth in Ralph C. Russell, *The Carlton Trail: The Broad Highway into the Saskatchewan Country from the Red River Settlement, 1840–1880,* rev. ed. (Saskatoon, Saskatchewan: Modern Press, 1956). For an excerpt see Ralph C. Russell, "The Carlton Trail," *Saskatchewan History* 8 (Winter 1955): 22–27.

Five Canada, Department of Energy, Mines, and Resources topographic maps 1:500 000 are helpful for the Fort Garry-Fort Carlton leg of the journey: Brandon-Winnipeg [Manitoba]; Indian Head-Brandon [Manitoba-Saskatchewan]; Broadview-Dauphin [Manitoba-Saskatchewan]; Moose Jaw-Watrous [Saskatchewan]; Saskatoon-Prince Albert [Saskatchewan].

SUNDAY, AUGUST 22, 1858.   Traded our last remaining American horse to Mr. Roan for an Indian horse. Mr. Sergeant and Hind came into camp during the morning, having stayed all night at Fort Garry. At noon we bid farewell to our host and hostess, as also Mr. Sergeant. Pulled up stakes and started. Camped at a small village on the banks of the Assinniboine. Roads good. Sloughs bridged. Character of the country low and flat prairie interspersed with thickets and timber of small growth. On the opposite banks is a heavy body timber of larger growth. This village which is situated at the foot of the Assinniboine Portage boasts of a Catholic church and a nunnery.[2] Here we were welcomed by Mr. Velpeau, a native of French descent, and to whom we were indebted for a bottle of Scotland's favorite beverage, "Mountain Dew." The feed here for our animals was excellent. The mosquitoes proved somewhat troublesome. Distance from Mr. Roan 13 miles.

MONDAY, AUGUST 23, 1858.   Passed the Portage trading post, a tributary of the Hudson's Bay.[3] Met a train coming in from the plains loaded with pemmican, buffalo robes, skins, and furs. Bought a dressed buffalo skin from one of the hunters which cost us about fifty cents. This skin we intended to make a boat of to cross streams. Bought a few articles at the post which we overlooked at Ft. Garry. Weather fine. Wood and water scarce after we left the post. Grass in the meadows is very rank. Camped on the prairie, without wood and water. Traveled about twenty-five miles.

TUESDAY, AUGUST 24, 1858.   This morning after we traveled about seven miles, we came across some water which brought quite a relief. Here we camped and cooked breakfast. While hitching, a hunter bound for the settlements [came into

[2] Present St. Francois Xavier. Thomas McMicking, *Overland from Canada to British Columbia. By Mr. Thomas McMicking of Queenston, Canada West,* ed. Joanne Leduc (Vancouver: University of British Columbia Press, 1981), p. 91n19.

[3] White Horse Plain or Lane's Post at Pigeon Lake. Ibid., p. 90n19.

camp], from him we learned that we were on the wrong trail and were then going to Swan Lake. We struck a bargain with him to take us to the right trail, giving him a shirt and two plugs of tobacco. We cut across the country and early in the afternoon came to it. The guide then left us, after giving us directions how to proceed to White Horse Plains.[4] We lost by this operation about ten miles. While cutting across the country we found plenty of high bush cranberries, and choke cherries. Wood and water plenty. Character of the country, changing for the better. Soil diversified. Travel on direct course, 25 miles.

WEDNESDAY, AUGUST 25, 1858. Road very bad. Met a train of eight carts of Bungee Indians[5] traveling north. Wood and water scarce. Arrived at White Horse Settlement, being the last on the route, about two o'clock. Here we found two Americans, one from Virginia and the other a Missourian. Occupied the afternoon in making axles for our carts in case we should have any breakdowns. Immediately upon pitching our camp, Hind, whose conduct as leader had become too overbearing and who took particular pains to vent his spleen on myself, kicked up a rumpus as usual and waded into my *affections*. For the first time we came to close quarters; and there is no knowing who would have had the best of it, had we not been parted by the rest of the company to offset his activity. I possessed the wind; and I flatter myself that in the end I would have worried him out. About half an hour afterwards he asked my pardon which was freely granted, and shook hands. His doom as a leader of the party was sealed, and upon Joe Houck

---

[4] White Horse Plains stretch along the Assiniboine River. Irene M. Spry, ed., *The Papers of the Palliser Expedition, 1857–1860,* Publications of the Champlain Society, vol. 44 (Toronto: Champlain Society, 1968), end map.

[5] Bands of Chippewa or Ojibwa in southern Manitoba were called Bungee by Hudson's Bay traders. John R. Swanton, *The Indian Tribes of North America,* Bureau of American Ethnology, Bulletin 145 (Washington: Government Printing Office, 1952), pp. 260, 551. Only less well-known tribal designations will be identified herein.

we put the mantle of authority. The funds of the company he still retained.

This village boasts of a windmill, like those of Ft. Garry. From these Americans, whose names have slipped my memory, we learned that a free trader by the name of P. P. Pambrun had started two days before with his train, and would travel the same route as we as far as Fort Pitt. Had a social time at the house during the night, most of the party "feeling their oats" before they ceased. Rained very hard all night. The distance from Fort Garry to this place is estimated at 65 miles.[6] We compute our travel this morning at sixteen miles. These two Americans are trappers and hunters, making a trip every summer to the headwaters of the Missouri and returning late in the fall to winter quarters laden down with the trophies of the chase. Both were married to Blackfeet women.

THURSDAY, AUGUST 26, 1858.   Road very muddy, trail very plain. Had quite an exciting scene in the afternoon, no less than a fight between Emehiser's dog and a full grown badger. As soon as we saw that the dog was getting the worst of it, we came to his rescue and finished him with a volley from our pistols. Character of the country, equal portions of prairie and timber with first rate soil, water plenty. Camped near a marsh. Traveled about 20 miles. During the night considerable frost fell.

FRIDAY, AUGUST 27, 1858.   Our road today lay through a low and willow swamp. Traveling very bad. Late in the evening we crossed a small running stream. Here the soil changed from rich black loam to sandy. Ascended a hill and found a beautiful camping ground. The surface of the hill was covered with rich luxuriant grass; while on the sides and nearly surrounding the hill was a heavy grove of pople; and at the western base a fine cool running stream. Traveled about 20 miles. Weather fine. Heavy frost at night. We are now sleeping

---

[6] Using this distance, the party was probably at Portage la Prairie.

under our carts, having no tents, as we had destroyed them to make blankets for our horses.

SATURDAY, AUGUST 28, 1858.   Character of the country quite diversified, level and undulating prairies interspersed with marshes. Sand ridges or hills covered with creeping cedar (Indian name, Cetah-upsis) and smoking weed (Indian, as-a-gach-a-pa-qua) with here and there a group of spruce pine, on one of which we found a blaze with "P. P."[7] marked on it. This creeping cedar and smoking weed was the first we have seen. Both are evergreens; and the ground in spots is thickly matted with it. Either one would make a magnificent border for garden beds. Saw a fox, gave chase, but soon eluded further pursuit. Passed several small lakes. Crossed three small running streams. Carried wood and water with us as we could not see any timber near after we got out into the prairie. Camped and found that we done well in bringing those necessaries along. Trail good. Weather fair. Traveled about twenty-five miles. No frost.

SUNDAY, AUGUST 29, 1858.   Character of the country unchanged. Passed several small lakes. Killed enough ducks to make a good meal. Wood and water plenty. Camped near some small lakes and pople groves.[8] Traveled about twenty-five miles. Weather fine. No frost.

MONDAY, AUGUST 30, 1858.   Character of the country low and marshy. Passed innumerable small lakes. On the road we plucked several sprigs that resembled anisette very much. Traveled about twenty miles and camped on the banks of the Little Saskatchewan or Rapid River.[9] This river is very deep

[7] See entries for 25 August above and 30 August and 4 September below.

[8] Pople is a variant spelling of popple or poplar.

[9] Contemporary maps sometimes used both names as Jones did here. Present day maps designate this river as the Little Saskatchewan or Minnedosa. It joins the Assiniboine about nine miles west of Brandon. Spry, *Papers of the Palliser Expedition,* end map; Russell, *Carlton Trail,* p. 8.

and rapid but not very wide. We drove our animals in and they soon swam across. The stream is about eighty feet wide and not fordable at any season of the year. On the opposite side we saw a skeleton frame made of willow. It fell to the lot of Emehiser to swim across and bring it over. While on the other side, he found a post marked by Pambrun who had crossed the day previous, having heard that we were *en route*. As soon as the skeleton frame was brought over, we covered it with our dressed buffalo skin and lashed it fast on the inside. The boat representing a canoe when finished and would hold from five to six hundred weight. When ready to launch, we fastened a rope to each end; and giving one to Emehiser he again swam across with the line, sending his clothes and another man. We soon had the pleasure of seeing our provisions and traps safely landed on the opposite shore.

It being late, we deferred crossing the carts till morning. Hind and myself staying with the carts and slept comfortably. During the night the boys shot a skunk. The report awakened us; and at first we thought we were attacked by Indians. Traveled about twenty miles.

TUESDAY, AUGUST 31, 1858.   Drawed our carts over by ropes. Loaded and started. After ascending the hill which is rather steep and long, we again passed through such country as yesterday. Continually passing lakes and pople groves. Grass very good. Weather cool and cloudy. Camped near a swamp and grove. Traveled about twelve miles.

WEDNESDAY, SEPTEMBER 1, 1858.   Morning travel presented us change in the features of the country. Afternoon, came to fine open prairies. Passed several fresh and salt water lakes. Killed a fine mess of ducks. Some of these lakes are a theme of study for philosophers and certainly are curious. Two lakes with but a small strip of land, barely room enough for one wagon to pass through—the one will be salt and the other be pure fresh water. The banks of one will be thickly encrusted with salt, the other bordered by grass and beautiful flowers, presenting quite a striking contrast. Some lakes not more than one hundred feet apart. One will be at least eight feet higher than the other. We saw three rising one above the other with less distance intervening. Wood plenty. Weather cool and cloudy. Traveled about 24 miles.

THURSDAY, SEPTEMBER 2, 1858.   Country low and swampy again, trail very bad. Crossed several deep running sloughs. Passed early this morning a very large lake to the right. Came very near of having a serious difficulty with Hind. I was very sick for awhile this morning. The boys took the difficulty out of my hands and gave Hind to understand that they didn't want to hear any more from him during the remainder of the trip. Weather cold and rainy during day and night. Traveled about twelve miles and camped near a clear running stream on a small clear spot of prairie. Wood plenty.

FRIDAY, SEPTEMBER 3, 1858.   Trail during morning travel very bad, afternoon better. Character of the country unchanged. Crossed Bird Tail Creek and another small stream, name unknown, near which we camped. Experienced heavy wind and rain. Traveled about twenty miles. Wood and water plenty. Grass good.

SATURDAY, SEPTEMBER 4, 1858.   Traveled about eight miles and came to the crossing of the Assinniboine River. The descent is precipitous and bad. The traveling during the morning was fair. Upon arriving at the margin of the river we discovered that the ferry, belonging to the Hudson's Bay Company, was on the other side. As the river was cold, we cast lots who should swim across and pull the flatboat over. It fell to the lot of Jas. E. Smith of our mess. Over he went; and we all crossed in three crossings. As the last load was coming off, three half-breeds, attaches of the fort, having seen before we descended the banks came and met us with the intention of bringing the boat across.

Leaving the river we wound around the foot of the hill. We

Fort Ellice
From Manton Marble, "To Red River and Beyond," Harper's New
Monthly Magazine 21 (October 1860)

finally ascended in somewhat circuitous route, some portions of which was very steep and bad. After arriving at the summit we proceeded about half a mile and came to Fort Ellice. This fort is situated on a high table land at the confluence of the Assinniboine River and Beaver Creek.[10] It has a fine commanding position of the surrounding country and could when necessity compelled resist a large army of savages. At the fort we saw quite a number of Indians of the Rabbit Skin tribe.[11] Here we caught up with Mr. Pambrun's train, consisting of ten carts, himself and three half-breeds, bound for Red Deer Lake situated about 200 miles north of Fort Pitt. Fort Ellice is under the supervision of Wm. McKay, from whose hands we received a welcome. Bought another dressed buffalo skin, some marrow, fat, etc. In one of the yards belonging to the fort we noticed a fine buffalo cow, quite domesticated.

After dinner we formed a junction with Pambrun's train. Here also we were joined by Mr. Louch, an English gentleman, who was on a hunting tour, expressing a wish to spend the winter in hunting in the vicinity of Fort Pitt or Carleton and return to Merry England in the spring. Sold one of our carts to Angus McKay for two guineas, or $10, which is all that they are worth. The country through which we passed through this afternoon is similar to that on the opposite side of the river. Camped near a swamp where there was plenty of wood, water, and grass. Rained hard during the night; and we all got soaking wet. Distance traveled during the day about sixteen miles.[12]

[10] Jones reckoned this as eight miles downriver from present St. Lazare, Manitoba, at the junction of the Qu'Appelle and Assiniboine rivers. See entry for 5 September below.

[11] A band of Plains Cree was known as Wabuswaianuk or Rabbit Skins. Swanton, *Indian Tribes of North America*, p. 554.

[12] Although no modern roads follow major segments of the trail, from here to Touchwood Hills and beyond the Grand Trunk Pacific Railway, eventually merged into the Canadian National Railway, was constructed approximately following the Carlton Trail. Russell, *Carlton Trail*, p. 12.

The post journal noted that "A party of Americans arrived here on there

JUNCTION OF THE ASSINIBOINE AND QU'APPELLE RIVERS.

Junction of the Assiniboine and Qu'Appelle Rivers
From Manton Marble, "To Red River and Beyond," Harper's New
Monthly Magazine 21 (October 1860)

SUNDAY, SEPTEMBER 5, 1858. This morning we passed through rocky and gravelly prairie for eight miles till we came to Qu'Appelle or Calling River. This river is small and barely fordable. It is skirted by timber; and here is the last oak you will see on the route. The descent to the river is very bad and precipitous. On arriving at the bottom, Mr. Pambrun looked out for a ford, as the water was too deep at the regular ford. Finally they found one, and, by cutting down the banks on the opposite side, made a tolerable ford. Our carts being heavily loaded we had to wade it, the water being very cold. It occupied all the afternoon in crossing. We camped near the banks. Rained all day and night. Distance from last night's camp 8 miles.

MONDAY, SEPTEMBER 6, 1858. It took us all morning to ascend the hill, having to double teams, the hill being very bad and long. Character of the country on top of the hill similar to what we passed through. Passed several lakes. Killed a fine mess of canvasbacks and teal. Heavy winds and rain all day and night. Trail good. Camped as usual on the prairie near lake and grove. Traveled about 15 miles.

TUESDAY, SEPTEMBER 7, 1858. Trail still continues to be good notwithstanding the rains. Crossed Broken Arm Creek[13] early in the morning. Crossing good. As usual killed a fine mess of ducks. Wood and water scarce. Country rolling prairie. Soil of different qualities. Wind and rain all day. Traveled 20 miles.

WEDNESDAY, SEPTEMBER 8, 1858. Again crossed Broken Arm Creek. Crossing good. Character of the country unchanged. Soil sandy and pebbly. Heavy winds and rain. Trail

[sic] was goin[g] across the Mountains." It further mentioned their departure the following day. Hudson's Bay Company Archives, Provincial Archives of Manitoba, Fort Ellice Post Journal, 1858–1859 [1864], B.63/a/4, microfilm, reel 1M51.

[13] Cutarm Creek.

bad towards the close of the afternoon. Wood scarce. Had to carry wood with us. Water plenty. Good feed for animals. Traveled 20 miles.

THURSDAY, SEPTEMBER 9, 1858.   Traveled through prairie all day with the characteristic soil of yesterday. Trail fair. Had to carry wood with us. Wood being very scarce along the route. Crossed a running stream. Camped at night near a lake. Heavy wind and rain all day. Distance 23 miles.

FRIDAY, SEPTEMBER 10, 1858.   Trail very bad. No change in the features of the country till noon. Came to groves. Crossed two lakes, one running stream and numerous sloughs in the afternoon. The lakes were deep, coming up to the cart beds. As usual had to wade. Killed a fine mess of ducks. Saw several skunks. Passed a large field of wild roses in full bloom which was gladsome to the eyes. It reminded us of what we left behind us. Camped near a slough and grove. Traveled about twenty miles. Weather fair. During the night it froze the water in our buckets to the thickness of a pane of glass.

SATURDAY, SEPTEMBER 11, 1858.   Trail bad. Crossed three lakes and numerous sloughs. Depth of lakes 2½ feet. Country changed from undulating to hilly. Numerous lakes on both sides of the trail. As usual, a mess of ducks. Weather clear and pleasant. Camped near lake and grove. Traveled 22 miles.

SUNDAY, SEPTEMBER 12, 1858.   Features of the country same as yesterday. Crossed two lakes and several sloughs. This morning Mr. Pambrun presented us with a dish of boiled skunk. It was tempting to look at. We all tasted of it, but couldn't go it.

"You may bake, roast and broil, if you will,

The scent of the skunk will hang round it still."
Vile parody on Tom Moore.[14]

The odor was too strong. We cast it aside for our pemmican rubbaboo made of flour and pemmican boiled. The half-breeds consider a skunk a great luxury and will set aside all other meats, taking it as a preference. For my part, I could not find it palatable; and as for the *scent,* imagine for yourself.

Weather fair. Wood and water plenty. Camped near a lake and grove. Traveled about twenty-five miles. Night being clear, we saw for the first time the Great Comet near the Polar Bear. It presented quite a brilliant appearance. It excited considerable curiosity with Pambrun's half-breeds, as well as ourselves. Judging from their physiognomy, they were afraid that some dreadful calamity was impending and about bursting upon them. It was in vain that we tried to quiet their superstitious fears.[15]

MONDAY, SEPTEMBER 13, 1858. Country very rough and hilly especially in the vicinity of Fort Touchwood Hills[16] or

[14] Suggestive of the closing lines of the first stanza of Irish poet Thomas Moore's (1779–1852) popular *Believe Me, If All Those Enduring Young Charms:*

> Let thy loveliness fade as it will;
> And around the dear ruin, each wish of my heart
> Would entwine itself verdantly still!

[15] Jones noted the comet several times for a month; his last mention was made 13 October. Donati's comet attracted world-wide attention and has since become standard textbook fare. Robert Stawell Ball, *A Popular Guide to the Heavens: A Series of Eighty-Six Plates with Explanatory Text and Index,* 4th ed. (London: George Philip & Son, 1925), p. 21 and plate; Fred L. Whipple, "The Rotation of Comet Nuclei," in *Comets,* ed. Laurel L. Wilkening (Tucson, Ariz.: University of Arizona Press, 1982), pp. 227–250.

[16] The Touchwood Hills Trading Post was situated at the junction of two trails. Spry, *Papers of the Palliser Expedition,* end map.

There is no trading post journal for this date in the Hudson's Bay Company Archives, Provincial Archives of Manitoba. Judith Hudson Beattie to author, August 19, 1987.

Touchwood Mountains. Arrived at the fort about the middle of the afternoon, and camped about a mile from the fort. Distance from last night's camp about fifteen miles. Weather fine and clear. Wood and water plenty.

The fort is situated on an open table land and does not hold a commanding position. It is built of hewed logs same as Fort Ellice. It is under charge of Mr. Taylor, a young man and a kind and courteous gentleman in every respect; and to him we [were] under many obligations.

A large band of Puppees[17] and Rabbit-skins, tribes of the Crees, had just come in from a successful hunt and were encamped all around the fort. Near our camp their horses were pasturing. I have never seen a finer band of horses anywhere nor a greater variety of colors, calico horses of almost every hue; and they looked as sleek as if they had been curried down for the last six months. The chiefs and head men paid us a visit. The head chief presented us with three bladders of marrow fat and a panful of service, or mis-as-qui-tom-i-ca berries.[18] From Mr. Pambrun, who could talk their language fluently and who acted as our interpreter, they learned where we were from and to where we were bound. They seemed much surprised that such a small party should undertake such a trip.

As the chief made us a present he of course expected one in return which we gave in the shape of tobacco. We invited the chief and one or two others to sup with us; and we feasted them with pork and beans with which they seemed delighted, especially the beans. After supper we circulated the pipe, taking a few whiffs and then passing it on to the next, and so on till the pipe was empty. They appeared much pleased at our

[17] This may have been a band of Plains Cree sometimes called Little Dogs. Swanton, *Indian Tribes of North America,* p. 554. See note 11 above.

[18] A corruption of misaskwatomin, the Cree word for the fruit of the misaskwat, the tree of much wood. The service berry is also known as the Saskatoon. Frederick Webb Hodge, ed., *Handbook of American Indians North of Mexico,* Bureau of American Ethnology, Bulletin 30, 2 vols. (Washington: Government Printing Office, 1907–1910), 2: 468.

sociability; and when they retired, the chief appointed a vener-
able old man to stay in our camp all night to watch any of the
young braves that came around and to see that nothing was
stolen from us.

I had never seen an Indian before but what wore some article
of Anglo-Saxon manufacture; but here you could see a great
many. No cloth bound their loins or covered their nakedness.
The skin dressed from the trophies of the chase was used and
manufactured into a shirt and decorated in true barbaric style.
No brass or silver rings hung on their ears or glass beads
around their necks; but eagle's claws and beads made from
the muscle [sic] shell were put in requisition, the buffalo robe
fantastically painted with red and yellow, which is found in
large quantities on the Assinniboine and its tributaries, the
bow and quiver of arrows instead of the gun. A great many of
them, however, were dressed in Hudson's Bay clothing, and
sported an half ounce ball gun, and aped the manners of the
whites as much as possible.

The Indian and half-breed hunters when hunting buffalo
load their gun while on a full run. They take out a ball, put it
in their mouth, take their powder horn, pour what they think
is a charge down the muzzle, drop the ball in without any
wadding, and as all their guns are flintlocks they pour a little
in the pan. They can load and fire in this manner in an incredi-
ble short space of time.

We kept watch all night. Upon the least little noise made,
the old brave who was lying wrapped up in his robe by the
fire would instantly raise himself and peer around. The least
unusual noise would start him; but the movements of our night
watch he seemed to take no notice of. His sense of hearing must
have been very acute; for he would at times rise when I didn't
hear anything. The chief was a large noble looking Indian;
and by the manner in which he ordered the braves around I
should judge that he was the "boss of the shanty." These bands
of Indians a few days before our arrival drove a herd of buffalo,
killed and captured three hundred and eighty-seven.

The service or mis-as-quitomica berry both in color and taste and forms in a dried state [is] one of the staple articles of food. It is indigenous to the soil, and grows in abundance.

TUESDAY, SEPTEMBER 14, 1858.   Traded this morning with the Indians. Procured a supply of marrow fat and service berries. Mr. Pambrun astonished the natives during breakfast time by shooting a goose on the wing. Mr. Pambrun, procured fresh horses from the Indians, giving the difference in rum, tobacco, and clothing. Bidding adieu to Mr. Taylor and the chiefs, we started at noon. Passed through very rough country. Camped for supper on a flat piece of prairie near a running stream.

After supper, Mr. Pambrun, entertaining the idea that some of the Puppees who are noted for their thieving propensities would follow us, gave the order to put [out] our fires and scatter the brands, which we did. Having formed in line, we took an oblique course from the trail. I should have stated that a portion of the train under the direction of one of Mr. Pambrun's half-breeds kept the road for some distance and had orders to leave the road at a certain point and form a junction with the main body. This was done in order to blind the Indians should they pursue us. The rear cart was to keep a strict lookout all during the march. A little after nine o'clock, both bodies met and proceeded together for some distance, till we came to a small spot of prairie almost entirely surrounded by willow brush, and pitched our camp forming our carts into a kraal. Our animals we picketed. Built no fires and made no noise. Most of the water we saw today was unfit for use, being alkaline and saline. The water at our previous camp was good. No disturbance or cause of alarm took place during the night. Weather clear and windy. Traveled about fifteen miles.

WEDNESDAY, SEPTEMBER 15, 1858.   The trail today led through a vast plain with a number of alkaline and saline lakes on each side. It being Jim Smith's birthday, we determined to have a good dinner and eat our last jar of preserved strawberries, a gift from Mrs. Cavalier of Selkirk Settlement. In this we failed for everything was spoiled by the bitter water which we had to use. Mr. Pambrun presented us with about a pound of good butter which was relished exceedingly. Had to carry wood with us. Camped at evening near a fresh water lake. Weather clear and sultry. Night cool and pleasant. Traveled about 20 miles. Soil of country poor as a general thing.

THURSDAY, SEPTEMBER 16, 1858.   Traveled about twenty-five miles. No change in the features of the country. Passed several fresh water lakes. Saw two beautiful rainbows as the sun was rising. Still carrying wood with us. Encamped near fresh water lake. Weather fine. Night cool and pleasant. Feed still continues good for animals. Killed a mess of ducks.

FRIDAY, SEPTEMBER 17, 1858.   Came to timber of small growth about 10 o'clock. Entered the plains again in the afternoon; and late in the evening we camped at the base of the Big Hills range. Water scarce. Weather pleasant. Heavy frost at night. Traveled about twenty-five miles. From the time we came to timber till we arrived at Big Hills, the soil was rich, undulating prairie interspersed with pople and balm of Gilead groves.

SATURDAY, SEPTEMBER 18, 1858.   Passed over Big Hills. The trail through was very rough. The hills are covered with large boulders. At the base of the hills we again came into good country, rolling prairie dotted with lakes and groves. First day of Indian Summer. Passed three large beautiful salt lakes. Had considerable difficulty in finding our oxen this morning; and had it not been for Mr. Pambrun's kindness in sending out his men, we would in all probability have lost them. We allowed them to run loose. Camped in a valley girded on the right by the plains and the left by a grove of large pople. Lake near. Night rainy. Traveled about twenty-five miles.

SUNDAY, SEPTEMBER 19, 1858.   Country rough and rolling with very rich soil. Wood and water plenty. Trail good. Passed several fine large salt lakes. Wind and rain all day. Mr. Pambrun presented us with a pan of marrow fat and about a quart of molasses. The latter tasted quite refreshing. We reciprocated the favor by giving several messes of pork and beans. Traveled about twenty-five miles and camped at Lac au Chaine, or Chain Lakes.

MONDAY, SEPTEMBER 20, 1858.   Country still rough with excellent soil. Trail good. Traveled about twelve miles and arrived at the south branch of the Saskatchewan. The descent to the river is rather bad. Pitched our camp on the margin of the river. Made with the assistance of Mr. Pambrun a large willow frame and sewed two skins together and covered it. Crossed all of Mr. Pambrun's goods over before dark. The boat was capable of holding twelve hundred. Had to paddle across, as the river is about 600 feet wide. At night four Cree Indians came into camp, having tracked us from last night's quarters. Ducks for dinner and supper. Comet still visible.

TUESDAY, SEPTEMBER 21, 1858.   Occupied all day in crossing and finished about 9 o'clock P.M. Mr. Pambrun with his usual liberality gave us a side of Red Deer or Elk which he procured from the Indians who visited us. Hind felt like kicking up another fuss, because he would not be allowed to wade into the goose we had for dinner when some of our party were absent on the other side. He had to *weaken*. We are beginning to feel as though we didn't care how soon he left us; as we are heartily tired of his laziness, overbearing manner, and gluttonous habits. Experiencing beautiful weather. Tied our carts, one behind the other, and rafted them across. Had considerable trouble to get them over, as the current is very rapid. We had a beautiful view of the Aurora Borealis at night. Heavy frost. Camped on the opposite margin of the river.

WEDNESDAY, SEPTEMBER 22, 1858.   While loading up we saw an Indian on the opposite shore making a raft and soon came across. He did not come near us. Had considerable trouble in ascending the hill. Some of our ponies proved treacherous and balky; and to cure them as well as to get out of the dilemma, we took them out of the shafts and hitched a rope to the shafts and tied the end to his [sic] tail, after the Red River style. An infallible remedy to make them pull. Character of the country similar to that on the opposite shore. Passed Duck Lake in the afternoon. This is the largest lake we have seen yet and is a beautiful sheet of water. Camped near lake and grove. Traveled about ten miles.

Reading Sir George Simpson's report of this country in the *St. Paul Pioneer and Democrat,* stating that this part of the country resembled very much the parks in England, this we pronounce unqualifiedly false in every particular bearing no more resemblance than the garden of Eden does to a sandy desert. It is destitute of its majestic oak, beech, and maple that he boasts of. On the river a few birch may be found; but the rest of the timber and especially in this vicinity to which he refers to is composed of small growth of pople, balm of Gilead and willow. When Mr. Simpson wrote that report, I think he must have been considerably under the influence of Hudson's Bay Rum. Sir George has made his "pile" here and is still accumulating. Now that his travels are over and has left several lasting mementos of his presence in the country by a numerous dark-colored progeny who boast of having a baronet for a father, I wonder if Sir George thought of his offspring when he wrote that lying report. Some of our party, three, are English born and have traveled extensively in England; and they all agree to the falsity of the report.[19]

[19] Jones probably carried the proceedings of the St. Paul meetings concerning an overland route to the Fraser mines with him. They were reported in the local newspapers, especially the *St. Paul Daily Pioneer and Democrat.* The remarks Jones made in this entry appeared 10 July 1858. This is established by his account of the journey in his letter published in the *Faribault Central Republican,* 6 July 1859.

"The Governor's reputation for having a woman at every post is exaggerated, but he showed a flagrant disregard for fur-trade custom and formed a series of liaisons with young mixed-blood women whom he treated in a most

THURSDAY, SEPTEMBER 23, 1858.   Character of the country unchanged. Traveled about ten miles and arrived at Fort Carlton at noon.[20] The descent to the fort is very precipitous. The fort is situated on a small strip of table land about midway between the river and to the top of the hill. It is built of hewed logs set endways. It does not hold a very commanding position. The name of the person in charge has slipped my memory. We had to pay him about seven shillings sterling for the use of the company's boat to cross the Saskatchewan River.[21] There were but few Indians around, some three or four lodges all told.

Turned our two oxen loose while making preparation to cross. Having wandered off we searched the thickets in vain. Finally we had recourse to the Indians. Hired one for a plug of tobacco. Sent John Palmer out with him. Palmer says that the Indian could track them all the while; and thinking he could make considerably more, he stopped and intimated that he would go no farther. Palmer gave him to understand in unmistakable terms that he was not to be trifled with, especially by a redskin, by signs. Palmer further says that he tried in vain to discover their tracks on the fallen leaves but could not, and that the Indian was rapidly going, dodging here and there, till finally he came up with them. Palmer then gave him a pipe, with which the Indian seemed satisfied.

I was sick all day, had a bilious attack. During the night as we lay in camp on the opposite side of the river from the fort,

callous manner." Sylvia Van Kirk, *Many Tender Ties: Women in Fur-Trade Society, 1670–1870,* 1st American ed. (Norman, Okla.: University of Oklahoma Press, 1983), p. 161.

[20]   Fort Carlton was situated on the east side of the river a few miles north of the present settlement of Carlton. Russell, *Carlton Trail,* p. 7.

There is not a trading post journal for this date in the Hudson's Bay Company Archives, Provincial Archives of Manitoba. Judith Hudson Beattie to author, August 19, 1987.

[21]   Jones identified this as a "skin boat." *Mankato Weekly Independent,* 16 July 1859; *Chatfield Democrat,* 18, 25 June 1859; *St. Paul Daily Pioneer and Democrat,* 25 June 1859; *Faribault Central Republican,* 22 June 1859.

we were kept constantly awake by an Indian powwow over a sick child; and betwixt it and the rain we passed a very disagreeable night of it. The Saskatchewan at this point is about a half mile wide, shallow most of the way.

CHAPTER 3

A Rose in Bloom and Frosty Nights:
Fort Carlton to Fort Edmonton

[Leaving Fort Carlton, the Jones party, following the Carlton Trail which now approximated the course of the North Saskatchewan River, reached Fort Pitt nine days later. Here, near present Frenchman Butte, a few miles from the Saskatchewan-Alberta border, the free trader with whom they had been traveling left them for another destination.

Jones and his friends headed westward for Fort Edmonton. Four days into October they picked a rose "in full bloom," but they were reminded of the lateness of the season by frosty nights and snow. Traveling by compass and by trail, whenever they could find it, the men now had occasional misgivings and homesickness for companions.

They found enough game to sustain them, the weather modified, they occasionally happened on to the trail, and a few chance meetings with Indians and traders assured them their course was now a correct one.

Finally, on 18 October, they reached Fort Edmonton. There the party witnessed the Indian trade in action, gathered information on the trail ahead, particularly from leaders of an exploration party that had just come from the mountains, obtained more appropriate supplies for their journey, and traded their carts for pack animals.]

* * *

FRIDAY, SEPTEMBER 24, 1858.   The ascent is very bad and steep and occupied considerable time. Had to [use] double teams a portion of the way. Traveled about twelve miles. Carried wood with us. Country principally plains. Wood very scarce. Water plenty but brackish. Weather warm and cloudy. Mr. Pambrun took a hunt and came in loaded down with game. He gave us a fine mess of ducks. Thickety Mountains in sight.[1] Camped on the plains.

SATURDAY, SEPTEMBER 25, 1858.   Plains till we arrived at Thickety Mountains. We found the trail across the mountains very rough and covered with thickets. Wood and water plenty. Passed several lakes. One of our party while out hunting had the good fortune to kill a goose, which we dished up for supper. Weather cool and cloudy during the day and night. Traveled about 25 miles.

SUNDAY, SEPTEMBER 26, 1858.   Country very rough, rocky and destitute of wood. Had to carry it with us from noon camp. Water plenty. Passed Mus-qua-hahe pah-mah-ta-kat Lake, Anglicized "the lake the bear waded through." Camped in a valley near a running stream. Weather cold and rainy during the day and night. Traveled about 20 miles.

MONDAY, SEPTEMBER 27, 1858.   Country still rough and hilly. Crossed Pee-tee-qua-tah-nah Creek and hills at noon. Traveled about twenty miles and camp at a lake bearing the same name. Weather fine. Again indebted to Mr. Pambrun for a goose. We now live in style—game at every meal. The comet's "narrative" has greatly enlarged since last we saw it. We passed over very poor soil today.

---

[1] Thickwood Hills, west of Fort Carlton. Spry, *Papers of the Palliser Expedition*, end map.

Three topographic maps 1:500 000 issued by Canada, Department of Energy, Mines, and Resources, are of interest for the Fort Carlton-Fort Edmonton segment of the Jones account: Saskatoon-Prince Albert [Saskatchewan]; Wainwright-Battleford [Saskatchewan-Alberta]; Red Deer-Edmonton [Alberta].

TUESDAY, SEPTEMBER 28, 1858.   No change in the general features of the country. Wood scarce, water plenty. Passed Pike Lake[2] and saw Fort Pike[3] in the distance. It is now abandoned. Our oxen gave us considerable trouble again this morning. Mr. Pambrun found them about four miles from camp. Weather cool and windy. Met a few Indians this morning from an unsuccessful hunt of forty days. They appeared very friendly and accompanied us a short distance. Weather fine and cool. Came to plenty of wood late in the evening. Traveled about twenty miles. The comet presented a beautiful appearance tonight. Camped near a lake.

WEDNESDAY, SEPTEMBER 29, 1858.   Country more level but very poor soil. Wood and water scarce. Water plenty [*sic*]. Weather warm and pleasant. Passed the "Three Brothers." These are three large Balm of Gileads standing alone on a vast plain. Crossed Amis-ka-nak, Sepesis, a small running stream. Night beautiful and clear. Beheld a beautiful Aurora Borealis. Heavy frost fell.

THURSDAY, SEPTEMBER 30, 1858.   Character of the country, valleys rich with wood and water plenty. Ridges sandy and gravelly. Crossed English Creek. Weather fine. Traveled about twenty miles. Camped on a hill near English Creek. Had to take water with us. The comet shone more brilliant than ever.

FRIDAY, OCTOBER 1, 1858.   Country rough with diversity of soil. Traveled about eighteen miles. Weather cool and cloudy and rained at night. Wood and water plenty. Camped near A-la-de-as Creek which we crossed.

SATURDAY, OCTOBER 2, 1858.   The country this morning was very rough as we approached the Saskatchewan. I picked

[2] Pike Lake is Jackfish Lake. McMicking, *Overland from Canada to British Columbia*, pp. 65, 98n47.

[3] This may be Mr. Murray's Trading Post. Spry, *Papers of the Palliser Expedition*, end map.

up a wild rose this morning in full bloom and stowed away in my logbook. We saw several; and the sight was truly refreshing. It brought back the scenes of home. The garlands we were wont to weave to crown our Queen of Love and Beauty. At noon while eating our dinner we were surprised by a party of forty Cree Indians dressed and painted in gala attire. At first we felt a little alarmed; but as soon as we saw them extend their *paws,* our fears subsided. They were well mounted, and to see them capering and prancing around us while on our march was indeed picturesque. They escorted us to the fort, where we arrived about three o'clock.

Fort Pitt is situated on a table land of considerable extent on the north side of the Saskatchewan and holds a commanding position. It is built like the rest of the forts. Around the fort were scattered about 200 lodges of Indians just returned from a hunt. The hills were perfectly dotted with horses. Around the lodges might be seen numerous children and far more numerous dogs. On the opposite side of the river could be seen quite a village, awaiting their turn to cross over in the Company's boat. Some not caring to wait had piled their chattels on their lodgepoles in the shape of a raft, fastened it to a horse, drove him and the dogs in, plunged in himself as well as his squaw, and hung to the poles. We saw quite a number cross in this manner.

The fort is under the command of Mr. Simpson, a young man of decidedly "ain't I some" and one of the *mementos* that Governor Simpson, or Sir George, as he is better known, left behind him.[4] A baron is his father; whether legal or illegal, it makes no difference to him. To him we paid our devoirs, and requested that we might have the use of his boat to cross the river, which was readily assented. We detailed a part of our company to get the boat and cross over; but they had considerable difficulty in getting the boat.

---

[4] James Simpson. Arthur S. Morton, *Sir George Simpson,* pp. 159–160. See note 19, chapter 2, above.

Pambrun and his train had formed a junction with his cousin here, who had preceded him and was there in waiting. They pitched their camp about a quarter of a mile from the fort. They now were besieged by the Indians who wanted "firewater." He opened out his goods, rolled out the casks, knocked out the bungs, and commenced to deal it out in regular style. They handing in their furs, provisions, or whatever they wanted to trade and receiving in return its equivalent (in those parts) in rum. As soon as one got his tin pint cup full, he would rush to his lodge, take a drink and pass it around. It was not long before it seemed to me that the whole camp was drunk. They now took hold of us, shook us by the hand, caressed us. Greasy old squaws and young ones too put their arms around our necks in a most affectionate manner and *saluting* us as brothers. Decrepit old cusses would go through the same performance and then drop down in maudlin insensibility. We stood it like heroes for awhile; but we soon got sick of it as it was "too much of the good thing;" and furthermore, if we had stayed much longer, we'd had to *bunk* down with them, as they compelled us to drink whenever they did. Bidding farewell to Mr. Pambrun we took our leave.

Before the performance commenced, Mr. Pambrun bought one of our carts and harness, paying its value in provisions.[5] Mr. Pambrun's course from Fort Pitt was north to Red Deer Lake. On our way back we called at the fort; and seeing several bushels of potatoes which had been raised there, (latitude about 53° north) we induced Mr. Simpson to part with a bushel, charging us only a shilling which is about twenty-two cents in American money. Very reasonable. Much more so than in the states. Money is so scarce in this country that when they get a sight of a shilling they are willing to part with almost anything to gain possession of it.

---

[5] Marrow fat, dried buffalo meat, and service berries. *Faribault Central Republican,* 6 July 1859.

Shouldering our potatoes, we moved for the boat and found
it in waiting. The boat was large enough to carry all of our
chattels and carts too. Driving our horses and oxen across,
we soon crossed with the boat. No sooner had we landed
upon the opposite side of the river than the Indians came
rushing towards us and soon emptied the boat of its contents,
notwithstanding our expostulations; however, they did not
steal anything. We fixed our carts together; and as one party
were loading the other were picketing the animals; and hard
work we had of it in catching the obstinate brutes. I paid
one Indian a plug of tobacco for catching a horse that I
thought was mine. After I had completely run myself down
in trying to catch him and as soon as we got into camp, I
found that my horse had been caught and picketed. The
Indian laughed and the boys too. The joke was good, for I
came into camp completely fagged out and sweating like a
porpoise.

During the night we were constantly kept awake and
annoyed by the Indians, our camp being literally surrounded.
Some of the old men stayed in camp all night; and notwithstanding that we kept a sharp lookout, yet we found several
small things missing in the morning. The countless number
of dogs they had with them made night hideous with their
discordant howls. They would steal our loose moccasins and
eat them, destroy our animal gear; and everything in the
shape of leather or skin that they could lay their voracious
fangs upon was sure to go. The Indians never feed them;
and the only remuneration that these poor brutes have for
acting as beasts of burden is the refuse of game killed and
offal. I have seen these poor dogs so loaded down that they
were barely able to crawl; and still the merciless stick fell
with rapidity upon their already lacerated backs, a proof
conclusive that the heart of an Indian is adamant and not
susceptible to any kindly feelings or commiseration for the
dumb portion of creation. This modern Babel found a response on the other side in the drunken revelry around the

camp of Pambrun. The Indian drum and song added much to disturb our equanimity. If we ever cursed the Indian it was done that night to our heart's content.

The river at this point I should judge to be about a quarter of a mile wide, and clear. Heretofore, streams of any size were muddy, of which I will mention Red, Pembina, Assinniboine, Qu'appelle, Little Saskatchewan, North and South branches of the Saskatchewan. The comet shone very brilliant tonight. Distance from last night's camp about 12 miles.

SUNDAY, OCTOBER 3, 1858.   A portion of our company crossed the river this morning and procured a supply of pounded buffalo meat, marrow fat and service berries, and also instructions how to proceed to Fort Edmonton by Mr. Simpson.[6] I forgot to mention in my notes of yesterday that we met two Americans bound on the same trip—Brewster of Mankato, Minn., and Gibson of Woodville, same state.[7] They joined our camp today. Traded some little with Indians. Started at noon and passed a great many Indians coming in from the plains. Country very rough. Our course is now due west. Wood and water scarce. Weather during the day fine. Night frost and snow. Traveled about ten miles.

MONDAY, OCTOBER 4, 1858.   Character of the country unchanged. Trail very indistinct towards evening. Camped near a small stream name unknown. Shot an Indian dog which had followed us. We again picked a rose in full bloom. Weather during the day, cool and cloudy. Heavy snow fell during the night.[8] Traveled about twenty-five miles.

[6] There is no Fort Pitt trading post journal for this date in the Hudson's Bay Company Archives, Provincial Archives of Manitoba. Judith Hudson Beattie to author, August 19, 1987.

[7] *Mankato Weekly Independent,* 16 July 1859. Brewster only stayed with the group for fifteen days. J. J. Gibson became a permanent member. See entries for 3, 20 October 1858 below.

[8] To a depth of four inches. *Chatfield Democrat,* 18, 25 June 1859; *St. Paul Daily Pioneer and Democrat,* 25 June 1859; *Faribault Central Republican,* 22 June 1859; *Mankato Weekly Independent,* 16 July 1859.

TUESDAY, OCTOBER 5, 1858.   Stayed in camp all day. Sent parties to look for trail. Returned unsuccessful. Snowed all day. Stopped at eve. Night very cold and disagreeable. The snow is now six inches deep. The complexion of matters now look squally. Some of the boys are getting disheartened and decidedly homesick. And among that number I shall reckon myself.

WEDNESDAY, OCTOBER 6, 1858.   About a mile from camp we struck a trail and followed it for about twelve miles when we again lost it. We had now to use our compass, course due west.[9] Country still rough with lakes and groves. Geese and ducks plenty. Weather very cold and freezing both day and night. Traveled sixteen miles.

THURSDAY, OCTOBER 7, 1858.   Thawing some today. Carting very heavy. Snow clogging the wheels. Country still rough. Saw four herds of buffalo. First we had seen since leaving the plains of Minnesota. Spent most of the day in the excitement of the chase. Being novices in this kind of sport, we were a long time before we could capture one. We now replenished our larder with the choicest portions. Ducks and geese still plenty in the lakes.

As yet we have found no trail. Now that we are in the country where buffalo is plenty, our drooping spirits have revived to their wonted cheerfulness. Weather during the day warm and pleasant; night freezing. We are still sleeping with nothing but our carts to shelter us. We manage to sleep very comfortably as we have plenty of buffalo robes and blankets. The comet presented a magnificent appearance tonight. We traveled only five miles.

FRIDAY, OCTOBER 8, 1858.   No change in the features of the country. Saw plenty of buffalo and had hard work to resist

[9] They were told at Fort Pitt that they would probably lose the trail. If they did then they should set their course due west. *Faribault Central Republican,* 6 July 1859.

the temptation of giving them a chase. Still traveling by our compass. Emehiser had the good fortune to kill a fine elk and brought it into camp late in the evening. He was separated from us most of the afternoon. Weather very cold and freezing both day and night. Built a rousing fire and enjoyed ourselves with a feast of elk. All in good spirits but still wishing we were on the trail. The country here is perfectly alive with game.[10] Traveled about seventeen miles.

SATURDAY, OCTOBER 9, 1858.   Country we traversed today principally bushy and very rough. The grass under the snow has the appearance of not being injured much by the snow. Still traveling by the compass and taking a west course. Buffalo still plenty but gave them no chase. Cold and snowing during the day and night. Traveled about eighteen miles.

SUNDAY, OCTOBER 10, 1858.   Country very rough in the morning but more level in the afternoon. No trail yet. Saw plenty of wolves, buffalo, ducks, and geese. Killed a fine mess of ducks. Crossed a running stream about noon. Warm and cloudy during day and night. Traveled about fifteen miles and camped near a tamarack swamp, being the first we have seen. The snow not so deep and fast disappearing. Good feed for animals.

MONDAY, OCTOBER 11, 1858.   Country hills and plains with tamarack groves and swamps. Weather very pleasant and thawing. Traveled about fifteen miles and camped near a lake. Saw but little game today. The comet is gradually disappearing.

TUESDAY, OCTOBER 12, 1858.   This morning we found that we could not effect a crossing of the lake; and we were obliged to go around which occupied nearly all day; and though we

[10] Including plentiful deer and antelope. *Chatfield Democrat*, 18, 25 June 1859; *St. Paul Daily Pioneer and Democrat*, 25 June 1859; *Faribault Central Republican*, 22 June 1859; *Mankato Weekly Independent*, 16 July 1859.

traveled about fifteen miles, yet we did not make more than about three miles in a direct line from last night's camp. Saw but few buffalo today but plenty of swans, geese, and ducks. Still traveling by the compass. Country very rough and marshy. Wood and water plenty. The snow has not entirely disappeared. The weather was very warm today. Camped near a beautiful lake and found splendid feed for our animals. The comet still decreasing.

WEDNESDAY, OCTOBER 13, 1858.   Early this morning we detailed a scout to look for trail in a northern course. Country more level. Proceeded about a mile and a half and came to a well beat hunting trail going north. I was sent to intercept our scout, as we had found the trail. After half an hour's fast traveling I came in sight of them. Attracting their attention, I informed them of the track. They had found a cart track going west. Joining company, we followed it till it crossed the trail that the train we were on at right angles. We here awaited for them. Followed cart trail. Saw numerous ducks, geese, and buffalo all making their way south. Feed still continues to be good in places for animals. Traveled about fifteen miles and camped on the prairie near wood and water. Weather clear and pleasant during the day. Heavy frost at night. Comet still visible but fast disappearing.

THURSDAY, OCTOBER 14, 1858.   Country most of the way today was low and marshy. Trail good. Weather pleasant. Snowed some during the night. Met an Indian and his squaw coming in from the plains and bound for the fort. From him we learned by signs that we were on the right road, and that it would be *four sleeps* before we arrived there. Crossed a number of sloughs, some very bad. Camped near a tamarack swamp. The wolves and coyotes howled all around us during the night. Traveled about 22 miles.

FRIDAY, OCTOBER 15, 1858.   Our road today lay through willow swamps which was very bad traveling. Traveled about twenty miles. Feed still good in places for animals. Came across several patches of wild peas, our animals preferring it to grass. Weather cold and cloudy. Woke up in the morning with a white coverlid, having snowed about three inches.

SATURDAY, OCTOBER 16, 1858. No change in the features of this Godforsaken country. Trail miserable. Snowing lightly all day. Crossed two running streams and several bad sloughs. Overtook an Indian bound for the fort. Traveled about twenty miles and camped near a running stream. Night cold and cloudy.

SUNDAY, OCTOBER 17, 1858. Still no change. Road miserable. Met at noon a train of twelve carts from the fort bound for the plains for provisions. Had some conversation with the leader, a white man. Soon after leaving them, we met another train of four carts bound for Fort Pitt. They calculated to reach Fort Pitt in three days; and we inferred from that that we had been a long way out of our road. Crossed a small running stream with very steep banks and skirted with brush and straggling tamaracks. Traveled about fifteen miles and arrived at the banks of the Saskatchewan where we camped. The descent is good. We drove our animals to the top of the hill where there was good pasturage and picketed them under guard of two men.

On the opposite banks stood the fort[11] upon an irregular table land and surrounded by numerous Indian lodges. They spied our arrival and came over in groups and appeared to be friendly. We were also visited by Messrs. Hall and Hodges of Mankato who were waiting for us, having heard that we were on the way.[12] Several white men in the employ of Hudson's

[11] Fort Edmonton. *Mankato Weekly Independent,* 16 July 1859; *Chatfield Democrat,* 18, 25 June 1859; *St. Paul Daily Pioneer and Democrat,* 25 June 1859; *Faribault Central Republican,* 22 June 1859.

[12] J. J. Hall and G. W. Hodgson (Hodgeson?) may have been the two overlanders Jones reported who left Fort Garry in mid-August. See entry for 21 August 1858 above. *Chatfield Democrat,* 18, 25 June 1859; *St. Paul Daily Pioneer and Democrat,* 25 June 1859; *Faribault Central Republican,* 22 June 1859; *Mankato Weekly Independent,* 16 July 1859.

Bay Company also gave us a call. The Indians stayed around us all night and some stayed with the two men on the hill. Their object for doing so we could not fathom, unless it was to watch and see that nothing was stolen from us; and I am inclined to think that such was the case, for if they wanted to plunder us they could have easily done so. Nor could we expect any assistance from the fort.

MONDAY, OCTOBER 18, 1858.   A part of our company crossed the river to visit the fort. The ascent to the fort is rather precipitous, but when once ascended is a gradual grade. It is situated on the north bank of the Saskatchewan. It is surrounded by hewed log palissade closely jointed and in the form of a rhomboid. It has towers mounted with small carronades.

We called upon Mr. Christie,[13] the chief Trader of the District and master of the fort, this being his headquarters. His manner during our interview did not favorably impress us. He looked and acted as though he was the "biggest toad in the puddle." Here also, we received an introduction to Capt. Palliser and Captain Blakiston,[14] British officers sent by their government on an exploring expedition. Capt. Blakiston having finished his labors was making preparations to proceed to Fort Carlton and winter there, and expressed his willingness to forward all letters we wished to send, an offer gratefully accepted. We intimated to Mr. Christie our desire of exchanging our carts and oxen for horses; and as he stood in need of both, he promised that he would attend to it on the morrow.

[13] William Joseph Christie. *Dictionary of Canadian Biography,* s.v. "Palliser, John," by Irene M. Spry.
[14] John Palliser's expedition was exploring British North America between 49° and 50° north latitude and 100° and 115° west longitude. Thomas Wright Blakiston had a scientific assignment with the expedition. Wallace, *The Dictionary of Canadian Biography,* 2:506; *Dictionary of Canadian Biography,* s.v. "Palliser, John," by Spry. For a detailed account see Irene M. Spry, *The Palliser Expedition: An Account of John Palliser's British North American Expedition, 1857–1860* (Toronto: Macmillan Co. of Canada, 1963); Spry, *Papers of the Palliser Expedition.*

Fort Edmonton, on the North Saskatchewan
By Permission of The Newberry Library

The Indian lodges we found here, consisted [of] Crees, Black-feet, Sursees,[15] and Stowees. They were waiting for the fort to trade with them. We visited a lodge where we heard a drum beat, and found it full of braves squatted on the floor, and in the center an incongruous mass of blankets, guns, knives, hatchets, tomahawks, pipes, tobacco, skins, etc., and in fact everything that an Indian is supposed to have. At the head sat the performer; while at his side sat the one beating the drum. The performer was making horrid grimaces, gesticulat-ing with his arms over his head and behind his back, moving them backward and forward, then coming in close contact as though he was exchanging some article from one hand to the other. When through he extended his arms with clenched hands till they all had guessed which hand the bone (for so it was) was in. Then the winners commenced to take their articles.

They are inveterate gamesters. From the time we arrived to the time we took our departure, which was on the third day after, they never ceased beating that drum; for when one was tired someone else was ready to fill his place as also that of the performer. I have been told from a person I have no reason to doubt and who is perfectly conversant with their customs and manners, that a gamester will after he has lost his horses, his lodge and the appurtenances belonging thereto, his dogs, blanket, gun, and even to the last stitch on his back, put up his hair against what he thinks it is worth, and that is the property he has lost. They are bound to give him that chance. However, I did not come across any that had their heads shaven.

While we were in, an Indian came in with about a yard of tobacco (it is twisted up like coil rope and all the stems taken out), counted the number of braves, cut them [sic] up into that many pieces, and distribute them, till he is no better off than

[15] The Sarcee or Sarsi of Athapascan linguistic stock were Blackfoot allies. Swanton, *Indian Tribes of North America,* pp. 591–593.

the rest. It is the same with liquor. What a lesson is taught here to the Anglo-Saxon race. But I must say that this is the only trait that I ever saw to admire in an Indian; and I have been in their midst for a number of years.

On the banks of the river about a mile below the fort, the company is supplied with a good article of coal, as it is found in considerable quantities. They burn it almost exclusively at the fort.

Capt. Blakiston took his departure at noon. From him we gleaned many items of interest about the route we were going to take. He went down the river in one of the Company's boats. We were told by everyone here that it was a dangerous undertaking to cross the Rocky Mountains at this season of the year, and that by no means could we cross them at the Jasper House Pass with animals. Furthermore, that if we overcame that formidable barrier there was no trail to Fraser River on the other side of the mountains, as the Company always left their animals at Boat Encampment on the west side and proceeded down the river in boats. Finding this to be the case we abandoned the idea of crossing them at that point and concluded that we would try the Sinclair Pass.[16] We tried today to procure a guide and partially succeeded. Hind, Brewster, and Sanford having concluded that they would stop and winter at Devil's Lake Settlement about forty miles distant from Edmonton.[17] As far as Hind was concerned, nothing could have pleased us better.

We found quite a camp of "freemen" on the west end of

[16] The plan was to proceed from Sinclair Pass to Colville Valley. *Chatfield Democrat,* 18, 25 June 1859; *St. Paul Daily Pioneer and Democrat,* 25 June 1859; *Faribault Central Republican,* 22 June 1859; *Mankato Weekly Independent,* 16 July 1859. See map, D. Geneva Lent, *West of the Mountains: James Sinclair and the Hudson's Bay Company* (Seattle, Wash.: University of Washington Press, 1963), p. 142.

[17] Hind and Sanford were members of the original party. Brewster had joined the group only fifteen days before.

the fort. "Freemen" is a term applied to all whites and half-breeds who are not in the employ of the Hudson's Bay Company. The salary of a Master of a Fort for the first three years is £75 per annum and his rations, after three years £100 and rations. The remainder of the employees only receive from £17 to £25 during their term of service, which is three years; and out of this if they want any flour, tea, or sugar, tobacco, etc., it is deducted out of their wages; so that at the end of the year there is nothing coming to them. Their rations is only three pounds of pemmican and seven pounds of *green* or fresh meat per day. These poor unfortunate devils are picked up in the north of Scotland and in Canada and are induced to come to this wilderness with flattering offers. When once they have got them on the Saskatchewan River, they stand a poor show to run away from the tyranny to which they are subjected by those pampered bastards of English barons who are in power. At the end of three years the Company is bound to take them and pay their passage to where they came from.

We had several applications from these employees to take them; but we could not; nor did we dare to do so, for if caught the merciless would put the Indians upon our track and "wipe us out," as the trappers say. Quite a number of them had made threats to run away upon the first opportunity; but I am afraid that opportunity will never present itself. These officials know very well whom they are dealing with. I have sat and listened to the wrongs and outrages they have received at their hands till my heart throbbed with indignation; but we were powerless and unable to extend a helping hand.

The Indians came around as usual to our camp, among whom were some chiefs whom we invited to sup with us. A party of half-breed hunters started out this morning and returned this evening loaded down with white rabbits. They were kind enough to give us a mess. The thickets are perfectly full of them. We were too busy with our own affairs to take the trouble of hunting them. The river here is not more than a hundred yards wide at low water and is very clear.

TUESDAY, OCTOBER 19, 1858.   Crossed the river and again paid a visit to Mr. Christie in order to consummate a trade. Plead business and put us off till tomorrow. Had a conversation with Capt. Palliser, who gave us considerable information as to what route we should take as also the manner of packing our horses, etc. He had been through Sinclair Pass and had blazed the path clear through. I read in an article since my arrival that Palliser had found a pass and was named after him. This I presume is a mistake, as he informed me that he had only gone through Sinclair Pass (an old Indian hunting trail) and recrossed the mountains at the Kootenay Pass near the boundary line about one hundred and fifty miles south of Sinclair's. Sinclair and his train was the first train of civilized folks that ever passed through, and hence it was so called; and it is not just that he should assume to name it after himself, because he also took a party through and blazed the way. Sinclair done the same himself.

We took several things that we couldn't pack and traded them with the "freemen" for such things as we needed, such as packsaddles, lariats, buckskin to make moccasins, etc.

About noon we saw the flag of St. George fluttering from the fort and accompanied by a discharge from one of the carronades as she was hoisted. Our bump of adventure being strongly developed, we soon made our appearance at the fort. Gazing on the proceeding for awhile our attention was soon drawn to a feature more interesting. A large band of Blackfeet Indians were running to and fro, dressed in their gala attire, bedecked profusely with Indian ornaments, and painted in the most approved styles. Meeting an intelligent looking half-breed, we inquired the cause of so much commotion in and around the fort. He informed us that they were making preparations to trade with the Indians; and on the other hand they

were preparing to meet the great Gy-as-cu-tus. Quite a number of the Indians wore the detested scarlet uniform of the
British, and with which they seem to be proud. The chief
also wore a scarlet coat, but extensively fringed with gold
embroidery, this being the distinction. He also flourished a
dress sword which was considerably rusty from exposure. No
marshal was ever more elated upon receiving his baton than
this *red-nigger* was with carrying his antique pattern sword.

The announcement being received by the Indians that the
Master of the fort was now ready to receive them, they formed
themselves into an irregular line with the chief at the head
leading a horse as a present to the Chief Trader. At the gates
of the fort the Indians were received in due form by the Hudson's Bay officials. The Indian chief after a brief address presented the horse and received in return a military coat after
the same pattern he wore, as also an invitation to dine with
him (the chief only), which is considered a great honor. Not
understanding the proceedings we had recourse to our interpreter. He informed us that the chief was to be the recipient
of the periodical entertainment given to all the chiefs when
they called at the fort. The doors were now closed; and the
Indians dispersed. Our informant stated that while at the
table the chief is plied pretty freely with rum; and if in consequence he becomes somewhat obstreperous and obstinate,
they dose the rum enough with laudanum to put him to sleep;
and in this insensible and maudlin state he is turned out and
given over to his followers.

The gates are now closed, and the portholes are opened.
There is but just room enough to pass your hand through. The
furs are now rapidly passed through the aperture by the *thirsty*
Indians; and the rum is distributed in the same manner with
equal rapidity; and then follows a scene of drunken revelry
that beggars description. Braves, squaws, and children are all
huddled indiscriminately. Virtue and decency finds no resting
place while in their bacchanalian orgy. Such a sickening and
disgusting sight I never wish to behold again. And this is the

way that giant monopoly has accrued its present enormous wealth. This is British philanthropy with a vengeance. Sleep was banished from our eyes during the night. Bedlam had let loose and was on a "bender."

WEDNESDAY, OCTOBER 20, 1858.   Again called on Mr. Christie. Was told by one of his servants that he was busy in the office and would be at leisure in a half an hour. Waited an hour and a half. My patience became sorely taxed. I finally made up my mind that I would wait no longer. So inquiring where his office was and being shown, I soon appeared before his *august* appearance, and demanded no further delay, as time was precious with us; and if he did not wish to trade, it was immaterial to us, as there were "freemen" outside ready to take them off our hands at a good bargain. He jumped up in a passion, *took my measure,* and remarked, "Well, come on, I'm tired of dancing attendance on you." Says I, "Mr. Christie, I presume you call yourself a gentleman?" He answered in the affirmative. I then said, "Mr. Christie, I demanded this trade [in a] gentlemanly manner, carefully avoiding in giving offence. Now, I want you to talk like a gentleman, as you are talking to an American and not to any of your hirelings, for we Americans are not in the *habit* of listening to any braggadocio." I then bid him a cool adieu and turned on my heels.

He called me back, apologized for his hastiness, and then led me to [the] kraal where there were several horses. I picked out two fine horses and gave him in return four carts and an ox. I then took the horses over. The balance of the company also traded off their carts now that he was brought to terms.[18] Jim Smith traded his navy pistol for a horse. We also sold him two or three bottles of pickles and about twenty pounds of

---

[18] They also traded for some pack saddles. *Chatfield Democrat,* 18, 25 June 1859; *St. Paul Daily Pioneer and Democrat,* 25 June 1859; *Faribault Central Republican,* 22 June 1859; *Mankato Weekly Independent,* 16 July 1859.

dried apples, the last we had, and received in exchange flour and potatoes, the latter proving quite a relish.

We had considerable difficulty in procuring a guide but finally succeeded in hiring a half-breed named Rossette to take us across the mountains across the Kootenay Pass, having altered our intention of crossing at Sinclair's Pass. The conditions of the bargain were that we should pay him £10 down and the balance £30 at the Hudson's Bay Post on the west side of the Rocky Mountains. We were told by everyone that if we did not cross this season that we would be compelled to wait here until the following August, hence our haste to get away. Our party now consists of Messrs. J. L. Houck, J. E. Smith, J. W. Jones, J. Palmer, Wm. Amesbury, Ira Emehiser, and Jn. Schaeffter of Faribault; J. J. Hall, G. W. Hodgeson of Mankato, and J. Gibson of Woodville, all Minnesotians, making ten without our guide.[19]

[19]   The post journal made no reference to Jones or the other overland travelers. There is enough overlap in the post journal and Jones entries, however, to confirm the presence of the Jones party. Hudson's Bay Company Archives, Provincial Archives of Manitoba, Edmonton Post Journal, 1858–1860, B.60/a/30, microfilm, reel 1M50.

The Elusive Trail and Mountain Pass: Fort Edmonton to Kootenay Trading Post

[The Jones party was advised to cross the mountains immediately because the passes might not be open again until late summer of the next year. They decided to press on and hired a guide to lead them through Kootenay Pass.

A day out of Fort Edmonton, hearing news of deep snow in Kootenay Pass and hostile Indians ahead, they decided to go by way of Sinclair Pass. Jones is sometimes vague or confusing about the route they were taking, and the travelers did lose the trail and became confused as to their bearings. It is likely they were trying to follow the "Cart Trail" or "The Wolf's Trail" which would take them southward approximately by way of present Camrose, Ponoka, Red Deer, to the west of Cochrane, and into the passes through the mountains to the south of Banff.

Amidst confusion and less than satisfactory guide help, it can only be conjectured that the party went through one pass and perhaps through another before finding what was later confirmed to be the (North) Kootenay Pass. Over the Continental Divide and the international boundary, Jones and his friends reached the Kootenay trading post a few miles away.

They were optimistic that they could go on to Colville, so their stay at the post was only long enough to replenish supplies and trade a little at the post and with the Indians encamped there. The resident trader suggested that too long a delay would run the risk of having to deal with heavy snow, a common occurrence at that season. At the same time they should proceed with caution as tension from last summer's Indian hostilities had not entirely subsided.]

*   *   *

[WEDNESDAY, OCTOBER 20, 1858, *continued*.] Having packed our animals, we bid farewell to the three cowards and proceeded on our way in good spirits. As it was late when we started, we had only gone two miles and a half before night overtook us. Camped near a lake. Feed good. Kept a sharp look out during the night. Soon after we had camped a half-breed came in leading a horse. He informed us that he was sent to us by Mr. Christie with his compliments; and that he had let us have a horse which did not belong to him and had brought one in place of him. Examined the horse and found that there was not much difference in them. We let him have the horse.

THURSDAY, OCTOBER 21, 1858. Character of the country unchanged. Trail bad. Weather warm and cloudy. Met a party of half-breeds and Blackfeet in the afternoon bound for the fort. From our guide we learned that they were just from the Kootenay Pass, and that the snow in the mountains was four feet deep, also that the Americans and Blackfeet were at war. This item of news altered the complexion of things. Held a council and concluded that we would try the Sinclair Pass. Notified our guide of our intention and he appeared willing. Crossed Vermilion River, a small stream.[1] Traveled about twenty-three miles.

[1] Jones seems to be in error as to the name of this river, both because of its direction and its distance from Edmonton. It is more likely the party was following the "Cart Trail," sometimes designated "The Wolf's Trail," in a southerly direction out of Edmonton. Spry, *Papers of the Palliser Expedition,* end map.

Some, but not all, of the confusion which plagued the travelers as they left Fort Edmonton and penetrated the mountains can be cleared up by

FRIDAY, OCTOBER 22, 1858. No change took place in the features of the country till towards evening, when we came to a ridge of hills with lakes in the valleys in which we saw a few ducks and geese. Crossed three small streams. Weather cloudy and misty. Night same. Traveled about 27 miles and camped in a valley close to a lake and grove.

SATURDAY, OCTOBER 23, 1858. This morning soon after leaving camp and in descending to the plains, the guide informed us that there were Blackfeet ahead. This somewhat surprised us. It being very misty, and we could not see but a short distance. He fired off his gun. Told us to do the same and be sure to keep them dry, as we might want to use them. We accordingly done so and as soon as our firing had ceased we heard it answered some distance off.

We had not proceeded far before we were met by two Indians on horseback. The guide informed them that we were a part of Capt. Palliser's party. "King George's men," with which they seemed satisfied. They led us to their camp which contained about a hundred souls. The guide informed us that the two Indians who met us were two noted chiefs, "Bear's hipbone" and "Bull's Head." I do not remember their Indian names. They saluted two of our party who were pointed out by the guide as commanding the party, with a "kiss" on the cheek and showed us their "King George's" medal which they wore around their necks. They wanted to trade and as we had some horses very inferior to some they had, we intimated our desire to do so. We brought out our gallon keg of rum, pour out some in a cup, and passed it to the two chiefs. The pint cup proved too heavy for them. We effected a trade on fair conditions, give the difference in a half gallon of rum, a blan-

topographic maps 1:500 000. See Canada, Department of Energy, Mines, and Resources maps: Red Deer-Edmonton [Alberta]; Banff-Bassano [Alberta]; Cranbrook-Lethbridge [Alberta-British Columbia-Montana]; United States Geological Survey map, Montana.

ket, and a yard or two of cloth, and procured three of their best horses for three of our poorest.

As soon as the trade was effected, we again took up our line of march. Proceeding some little distance and out of sight of the camp, we diverged from the road and scattered ourselves but still keeping in sight of each other, by directions of the guide who entertained the idea that we might be pursued. In this manner we traveled for some distance. Sometimes we would almost make a circle around a grove or lake. This method of traveling was intended to blind our trail. Towards evening we formed again into line and struck a "beeline" for the trail, which we reached in time to camp which was near a small lake. We estimate the distance made today at 20 miles on our right course.

SUNDAY, OCTOBER 24, 1858. Traveling very bad. Crossed Battle River.[2] This stream is about thirty feet wide and fordable during low water. Wood and water plenty. No snow. Weather warm and cloudy. Traveled about twenty-five miles, and camped [near] a small stream and tamarack swamp.

MONDAY, OCTOBER 25, 1858. Character of the country unchanged. Trail bad. Crossed Blind[man] River. This stream is about fifty feet wide and fordable during low water. Saw several elk. Passed through miserable country today. Weather mild and cloudy. Traveled about twenty-five miles and camped on the banks of Red Deer Creek.

TUESDAY, OCTOBER 26, 1858. Country still very rough and bad, interspersed with morasses. Weather clear and pleasant. Came within sight of the Rocky Mountains early in the morning. They are covered with snow. They are still a great distance off. Crossed Red Deer Creek. Also crossed Red Deer River.[3] This river is about 150 feet wide and very shallow. Crossed with the ripples in an oblique direction. Camped about a half

---

[2] The party was apparently near present Ponoka, Alberta.

[3] At present Red Deer, Alberta.

mile from its banks. Aspect of the country changing for the better. Traveled about twenty-five miles.

Have a finer view of the mountains this evening. They are indeed formidable looking barriers. The guide recounted the most dismal tales of Indians and hunters being lost in the passes of the mountains during the winter months, and assured us that the probabilities were strongly in favor of our losing our lives should we persist in the present rash undertaking. All this, however, (subsequently, we found it to be too true) fell upon deaf ears. Our motto had been and would still be "Onward!" We noticed the guide was packing up his traps in a smaller compass than hitherto. Looked suspicious. Traveled about twenty-five miles.

WEDNESDAY, OCTOBER 27, 1858.   This morning upon leaving camp, the guide told us to keep the track, that he would go across the country and hunt and meet us at noon. We all thought that he was deserting us, and several were on the point of leveling their rifles on his worthless carcass, but on a second thought they desisted.[4] We are now on a bleak desolate prairie, fully two hundred miles from the nearest abode of white men and with no assurance that we are on the right track. Before leaving us, he drew our attention to a peculiar shaped mountain in the form of a dome, called by Indians, Wy-teek-coo-stk-wan, in English, "Devil's Head."[5] Kept on the trail till noon, and finding that the trail was going southeast being in direct antagonism to that we should take. Held a council and concluded to steer for the "Devil's Head" across the country.[6] Traveled about 20 miles and camped near a heavy body of timber and swamp.

[4] The guide did not return. "Before leaving us he showed us Sinclair's Gap." *Chatfield Democrat*, 18, 25 June 1859; *St. Paul Daily Pioneer and Democrat*, 25 June 1859; *Faribault Central Republican*, 22 June 1859; *Mankato Weekly Independent*, 16 July 1859.

[5] Devil's Head is a "craggy knob" to the northeast of Banff. Spry, *The Palliser Expedition*, pp. 143, 179; Spry, *Papers of the Palliser Expedition*, end map.

[6] The guide had told them the gap located near Devil's Head was Sinclair's Pass. *Faribault Central Republican*, 6 July 1859.

Saw a campfire at night which we judged to be about five miles off. Immediately upon the discovery we extinguished ours and kept a vigilant watch all night. We were told by the Blackfeet whom we met soon after leaving the fort that we would probably meet with a band of five hundred warriors on the road; and we thought that probably that this was one of their fires. Nothing further caused alarm the rest of the night.

THURSDAY, OCTOBER 28, 1858. Came to plains early in the morning. As yet we have found no trail. Have scouts out all the time looking for one. Crossed several sloughs and running streams. Wood scarce. Weather mild and cloudy. Traveled about twenty miles and camped on the plains.

FRIDAY, OCTOBER 29, 1858. Came through very rough country most all day. No trail. Crossed several small running streams. Saw plenty of elk, deer, and few bears but spent no time in hunting. Wood, water, and feed plenty. Weather cool and pleasant. Traveled about twenty miles and camped near a small river which we afterwards learned was Little Red Deer River. We are now coming into a heavy pine country.

SATURDAY, OCTOBER 30, 1858. Amesbury and myself and Jim Smith and Emehiser concluded we would hunt some. We had hardly gone half a mile before we lost the track and sight of the train. We did not pay attention to this as we thought that they would still keep on the same side of the river; but in this we were mistaken as we found on the following day. They finding that the country was too rough concluded that they would recross as it was more inviting on the other side.

Amesbury and myself kept company. We saw plenty of deer but had only one fair shot; but for some cause we missed, a thing very unusual. The country was literally alive with game. We could hear the unwelcome growling of the bears on either hand and seemingly quite close. Fears of ferocious grizzlies took possession of me; and I must honestly confess that I felt considerable trepidation, so much so that I fancied that I was laboring under the "Curse of the Swamp," y-cleped fever, and ague. I cannot say as to the feelings of my companion; but this we are assured, we made rapid tracks till we got out of hearing.

We now concluded to go [to] the river in a straight course and see if the train had gone that way, as we were but a comparatively short distance from last night's camp, having made a very circuitous route; and if they had kept on the course started they would have passed this point. We carefully examined the ground but found no tracks. Seeing a mountain ahead, we made for it in order to see if we could not get a glimpse of any sign. While on the way, Jim, who had parted from his companion, met us and we traveled together. We crossed a large tract of fallen timber. Having ascended the mountain, we fired a volley but elicited no response. We fired at intervals during the whole afternoon, climbed the tallest trees, hoisted the "flag of distress," but all proved unavailing.

During the sombre hue of eve, we kindled a large fire and also set fire to the top of one of the dead pines near. The day which had been pleasant now turned extremely cold and freezing. Not having killed anything and having neglected to stuff our pockets with grub, we commenced to feel the pangs of hunger. When night had cleverly set in, I noticed as I thought directly south of us a rising star. I drawed the attention of my companions to it. We watched it for several minutes, expecting it to rise in the heavens; but it remained stationary, and we came to the conclusion that it was the signal fire of our train. We now looked for Emehiser's fire but could see none.

We held a consultation as to whether we should try to reach there through the night. Smith was in favor of trying. Amesbury was waiting for my opinion. I resolutely refused. I would take daylight for it and would risk the forest ahead. Without moonlight enough to take us through, Amesbury coincided and Jim concluded to stay. The night was so extremely cold that we had to build two fires and tried to sleep between; but it was no use.

The train had traveled about eight miles; and finding that

we did not catch up with the train at noon as we promised, they prudently stopped and remained camped till we should join them.

SUNDAY, OCTOBER 31, 1858.   We started this morning from the mountain; and we had not proceeded far from the base towards the river before we came to a large area of fallen timber. Now we thanked our stars that we did not make the attempt, as it was difficult enough in daylight much less in a dark night. The river we found to be frozen over. We attempted to cross on the ice but got a good wetting. The river fortunately was very shallow. We now ascended the hill in a southward course and gained the forest which was also thickly strewn with fallen timber. We now heard report of firearms. Traveled southeast whence the report came. The firing was kept up; and we answered each volley. We reached camp at noon in our exhausted state.

They saw our signal fire the night previous and heard our firing; but as the wind was against us we could not hear theirs. The same thing occurred this morning. We could distinctly hear their firing; but [they] could not hear ours. Emehiser and ourselves came to camp almost at the same moment. We done justice to our meal. The boys had killed a mess of prairie chickens close to camp. Traveled about ten miles.[7] Night very cold.

MONDAY, NOVEMBER 1, 1858.   Soon after leaving camp we crossed a small but well beat track going southward. Concluded to follow it for awhile, but we soon lost the track. Came to open plains at noon, and during noon camp three Assiniboin Indians came in. They were very friendly. We set them out some provisions which they seemed to relish. By signs we made them understand that we wanted a guide; and they promised to furnish us one in the evening. After dinner Hall accompanied them to their camp which was about three miles

[7] They had followed "an old trail . . . till we could follow it no longer." Ibid.

off. Hall says that he was a subject of much curiosity among
them. They examined everything of American manufacture
very minutely. The Indians, he says, received him very cor-
dially and intimated their desire to witness the use of a re-
volver, having never seen one before. He accordingly set up a
board placed at a distance of about twenty-five yards; and
being a good pistol shot he blazed away as fast as he could pull
the trigger in order to astonish them. Fortunately he put every
ball through. The Indians made a rush and seemed greatly
astonished when they saw it.

Hall made them to understand that we all had one; and if
the Blackfeet troubled us that we could kill sixty of them as
quick as he fired that pistol. And as they were hereditary
enemies of the Blackfeet, they seemed delighted and expressed
their wish that we might meet them in order to diminish their
numbers, a wish that Hall silently did not reciprocate. These
Indians are very religious and of the Episcopal or Church of
England faith. They all have their baptismal name such as
John, James, Mary, Susan, etc. They have books printed in
their own language, which is by characters.

We struck Sinclair's cart trail in the afternoon as were
ascending a mountain. In descending the scene that presented
itself was remarkably beautiful. The valley of Bow River appeared like a beautiful lawn, the gorge we were passing
through high and precipitous, the snow capped summit of the
Rocky Mountains in the distance. The placid and mirror-like
Bow River flowing in serpentine form through the valley.
Antelopes and deer were seen here and there, bounding along,
frightened at our approach. Met a few Indian hunters[8] from

[8] These were the last Indians the party encountered before crossing the
Continental Divide. They were probably from the Assiniboin camp referred
to above.

In a notation at the end of the journal, Jones listed the "Names of the
different tribes we passed. East side [of the Rocky Mountains:] Chippewas,
Sioux, Salteaux, Bungees, Pillagers, Stonies, Surzees, Crees, Assiniboin,
Blackfeet." See note 5, chapter 2, above; note 14, chapter 3, above.

Chippewa or Ojibwa from the falls of Sault Sainte Marie, Michigan, were

whom we procured some fresh antelope meat. Crossed Dead Man's River at its junction with Bow River and camped on its bank.[9]

Hall and guide came into a camp in the evening. He was the whitest Indian I had ever seen and in fact even whiter than many half-breeds I had seen. He was fantastically dressed in buckskin which suit he did not retain long as Emehiser traded his almost worn out suit for them [sic].[10] Bow River at this point is very shallow and rapid. Traveled about ten miles. Wood, water, and feed for animals plenty. Weather pleasant.

TUESDAY, NOVEMBER 2, 1858. Country very rough. Our road lay principally on side of mountains. Passed the ruins of Bow Fort.[11] This fort was destroyed a few years ago by the Blackfeet. Wrote on a smooth piece of board the names of each one of our party and some comments, placed near the chimney to attract the attention of any passers-by. Met several Indians, all friendly. We gave our Indian guide a gun, some ammunition, blanket, and some few trifling articles with which he seemed satisfied. Saw plenty of deer and antelope. Plenty of trout in the river. Camped at the foot of the Rocky Mountains near Bow River. Traveled about twenty-five miles. Weather cold and freezing during the night. The mountain at the foot of which we are camped is very high and precipitous and apparently but a short distance from the "Devil's Head."

called Saulteaux. Stonies was an English translation of Assiniboin, meaning "one who cooks by the use of stones." Swanton, *Indian Tribes of North America*, pp. 260, 387.

[9] Dead Man's River is today's Ghost River. Ghost River enters the Bow River a few miles west of present Cochrane. Spry, *The Palliser Expedition*, p. 142.

[10] The guide agreed to take them over the mountains in return for a blanket, gun, shirt, and a few small trinkets. *Faribault Central Republican*, 6 July 1859.

[11] Old Bow Fort, the so-called Piegan Post, was an abandoned Hudson's Bay Company post on the Bow River. Spry, *The Palliser Expedition*, pp. 38, 126; Spry, *Papers of the Palliser Expedition*, end map.

WEDNESDAY, NOVEMBER 3, 1858.   Crossed Bow River in the morning. Passed several carts that had been abandoned. The river at the fording is about 150 feet wide, shallow but rapid. Ascended and descended an upland and came to a valley now fairly in the mountains. We are now following the [Kananaskis River,][12] a stream of considerable size, pure and clear. Crossed and recrossed several times. Traveled about sixteen miles. This valley is very heavily timbered with pine, spruce, hemlock, yew, etc. Weather pleasant. Guide killed an antelope in the evening.

THURSDAY, NOVEMBER 4, 1858.   Our path today lay through a dense forest with heavy windfalls, especially in the burnt district. Trail very rough. Amesbury killed an English mountain cock. Rather smaller than the native of England. Traveled only about eight miles as we had to use the axes considerably which delayed us. Snowed a little during the night.

FRIDAY, NOVEMBER 5, 1858.   Trail very bad. Still encountering heavy windfalls. Had to cut our way through for a considerable distance. Let our horses loose during the night to shift for themselves as the feed is scarce. Still following the river and continually crossing it. Weather pleasant during the day. Pleasant night very cold. Traveled about fifteen miles.

SATURDAY, NOVEMBER 6, 1858.   Left the river in the afternoon and ascended a high ridge on the left hand side. Traveled about twelve miles and camped near a very high precipice. It was dark when we stopped; and as we found a small lake with good grass, we stopped on account of the feed for our animals not dreaming that we were so close to a precipice. We were not more than forty feet off. If any of our party had wandered in that direction, he would certainly have went over as it was

---

[12] The Kananaskis is a tributary of the Bow River flowing in from the south between Ozada and Exshaw.

appallingly dark. Our guide was quite sulky today because we would not camp where he wanted us to.

SUNDAY, NOVEMBER 7, 1858. Ascended to the top of the ridge and came to a stream in our descent running in a contrary direction from the one we had hitherto followed.[13] Saw quite a number of white grouse, a beautiful snow white bird with red feet and eyes. So white were they that you could hardly see them as they alighted on the snow. We killed a mess. The meat is rather blackish and tough. They are very small. We also saw a few Rocky Mountain sheep but could not get a shot. The snow on the ridge was about four feet deep in places. The summit of the ridge presented a bleak and desolate appearance, while all around us as far as the eye could reach lofty and precipitous snowcapped peaks reared themselves in majestic grandeur. Traveled about twelve miles. Feed for animals very scarce. (My birthday.)

MONDAY, NOVEMBER 8, 1858. Traveled about 15 miles. Trail good in the valley. No snow. Picked three "blue-bells" in full bloom. Plucked and stowed them away in my diary. The sight of them was truly refreshing. Feed for animals very scarce. Saw several sheep and goats. Weather cold and cloudy.

[13] The party was apparently crossing the Continental Divide, the present Alberta-British Columbia boundary, over either the North Kananaskis Pass or the South Kananaskis Pass. Jones is not precise enough to determine which one.

The river is the Palliser, a tributary of the Kootenay River. The trail followed the Palliser to the Kootenay and along that river to the southward.

Just how far the party approximated the trail before losing it is impossible to determine from the Jones journal. His entry for 10 November below raises a doubt and his entry for 21 November below confirms confusion and wandering.

The several passes caused confusion and were imprecisely described by several before they were "systematically explored and recorded." Irene M. Spry, "Routes through the Rockies: Palliser's Precursors in the Passes Leading through the Rocky Mountains from the Headwaters of the Saskatchewan River," *Beaver* Outfit 294 (Autumn 1963): 26–39; Spry, *Papers of the Palliser Expedition,* end map.

TUESDAY, NOVEMBER 9, 1858.   Traveled about eight miles. Camped at noon. A party of four started out to hunt for some *mutton.* The sheep are very wild; and it is very rarely that you can get a shot. While they were gone, we saw on the opposite mountain a string of about one hundred ascending in regular Indian file. The hunters returned unsuccessful. Weather pleasant. Feed for animals good.

WEDNESDAY, NOVEMBER 10, 1858.   Traveled about twelve miles and came to the plains (as we now thought on the west side, and as he assured us) and saw buffalo. Having heard that there were no buffaloes on the west side of the mountains, the sight of these animals staggered us. We informed our guide by signs that we were doubtful as to whether we had come out on the west side. He informed us that we were (treacherous hound) and became indignant at our suspicions. Still having faith in him, we concluded to camp awhile and give the buffaloes a chase, but returned unsuccessful. Our animals were too much jaded and had suffered from the want of food. We moved our camp some distance farther and camped on the banks of the river. Warm and rainy all day. Feed, wood, and water plenty.

At night we had a little jollification to honor our release from the mountains. Brought out the half gallon of rum and a bottle of brandy which we had brought along for *medicinal purposes.* Sang songs, told tales. Conversed about our *loved ones,* our homes, and our future prospects. The Indian became pretty mellow very early; and while he was drunk, he would occasionally put his ear to the ground, jump up excited, and snatch his gun, and made signs to us that there were Indians close by. The first time he done so we were on the alert and stood ready to meet our foe with a warm reception. Finding that his alarm was groundless, he relapsed into his "happy state," sang Indian ditties, and accompanied with beating time on a pack saddle. It was late when we retired. Snow very heavy during the night.

THURSDAY, NOVEMBER 11, 1858. The guide left us this morning with the traps we had given him as per agreement, showing before he left the trail we were to take, and assured us that we could reach the Mountain Fort of the Kootenay in three days. We kept the trail for awhile noting its course at the time in case we should lose it, which we soon did and traveled on the course we had noted. The snow is about six inches deep. Hunters went out for buffalo in the morning but returned without a victim. Character of the country very rough and principally prairie. Traveled about seven miles and camped near a willow thicket and lake. Feed good.

FRIDAY, NOVEMBER 12, 1858. The guide came back much to our surprise at noon and intimated his desire to keep on with us which we readily and gladly assented. Passed several lakes. Guide brought us on the trail again. Saw plenty of buffalo, elk, and deer. Camped near a lake and willow grove. Weather mild and cloudy. Traveled about ten miles.

SATURDAY, NOVEMBER 13, 1858. No change in the features of the country and we are still skirting the mountains to our right. Saw plenty of buffalo, elk, and deer. A part of our boys gave the buffaloes a chase and succeeded in bringing into camp a good supply of fresh meat. Wood and water plenty. Good feed for animals under the snow. Traveled about 15 miles.

SUNDAY, NOVEMBER 14, 1858. Wood and water plenty as also game. Didn't hunt any. Weather cold and cloudy. Traveled about 15 miles.

MONDAY, NOVEMBER 15, 1858. Country still the same and are still skirting the mountains. Experienced cold heavy winds. Wood, water, feed, and game in abundance. Traveled about twenty miles. Saw a drove of about 20 deer.

TUESDAY, NOVEMBER 16, 1858. Still the same rough country. Crossed a river (which we thought to be a branch of the

Columbia) with a beautiful valley. Saw today for the first time a hare. We set the dog on him; but he soon left the dog out of sight. Wood scarce today. Camped on the banks of the river. Traveled about 20 miles.

WEDNESDAY, NOVEMBER 17, 1858. Traveled about 12 miles. Country more level, with scarcely any snow. Crossed the river twice today. Shallow fords. The guide caught a fine mess of black-speckled trout, as also some red-speckled. Game plenty. Wood scarce. Water and feed plenty. Weather very cold.

THURSDAY, NOVEMBER 18, 1858. Country still the same and still skirting the mountains. Crossed two rivers. Wood very scarce. Saw buffalo, elk, and deer. Gave the buffaloes a chase but without success. Traveled about 15 miles. Weather very cold.

FRIDAY, NOVEMBER 19, 1858. The guide from some cause to us unknown is now taking us on a different course, from SSW to NNW. Country unchanged. Passed a beautiful lake. Game in abundance. The country is literally alive with deer. Wood, water, and feed plenty. The guide killed a deer at noon but made sad work of it in cutting it up. He saved the entrails after stripping them and cooked them for his supper. Weather very cold. Traveled about 12 miles.

SATURDAY, NOVEMBER 20, 1858. Traveled about fifteen miles. No changes in the features of the country. Crossed two streams. Wood, water, and game plenty. Weather cold.

SUNDAY, NOVEMBER 21, 1858. Traveled about fifteen miles and again entered the mountains at the Kootenay Pass and camped near the summit.[14] We encountered snow from two to

[14] If Jones is accurate about the location and the distances traveled from here to reach the Elk River, the party was at the North Kootenay Pass, near present Flathead, British Columbia. Upon reaching the Kootenay Trading Post they were informed by the trader that they had crossed the Kootenay Pass. Spry, "Routes through the Rockies"; Spry, *Papers of the Palliser Expedition,* end map; Spry, *The Palliser Expedition,* map 3, map 4; *Faribault Central Republican,* 6 July 1859.

fifteen feet deep. The snow in many places had drifted to such a height that there was no telling what depth it was. We turned the horses out where the snow was, not very deep; and we had to keep a constant watch to prevent them from going back.

Where we pitched our camp the snow was about fifteen feet deep. We cut a large hole through; gathered a few dry sticks and kindled a fire; and although we had good shelter yet the cold was so intense that sleep was out of the question; and we hugged the fire as close as we could. We had to relieve guard about every fifteen minutes. The poor animals must have suffered. There was not a particle of vegetation visible; and there they stood shivering in the merciless wintry blast. We covered them with all we could spare, but it was not enough. The thoughts that passed through our minds in rapid succession during that fearful night can be better imagined than described.

MONDAY, NOVEMBER 22, 1858.   With the first hint of morn, we disengaged the shovels from the packs and started. For the first few hundred feet we had very hard work in shoveling out a path for the horses through a tremendous snow drift, the Indian all the time gazing with amazement. After we got through the snow drift, the danger was not over through the gorge we had to pass through. Old Boreas had cleared the snow for a considerable distance; and it presented the appearance of a glacier. The balance of the way was steep and rocky and covered with ice; and it was with great difficulty that man and horse could keep their feet. The wind blew fearfully cold through the gap; and if [it] had not been for the amount of labor we had done and were doing, we would have frozen to death in a short time. Finally by great exertion we gained the gap, and made our descent rapidly to the valley below which we finally reached in the afternoon, and camped where there was scarcely any snow. Traveled about seven miles. Feed very scarce. Weather mild and snowing.

TUESDAY, NOVEMBER 23, 1858. The guide was sulky again today and wanted to go back. Spent the greater portion of the day in looking for the trail. Followed the guide through an almost impenetrable forest; and in some places we had to cut our way through. Weather mild and snowing. About four miles today. Crossed a stream numerous times; and each time we had to wade. The stream was very difficult to cross as it was frozen at the bottom.

WEDNESDAY, NOVEMBER 24, 1858. It was with considerable difficulty that we could get the guide to start this morning; and the only inducement that made him start was the promise of the best horse in the company. I had forgot to mention that before we entered the mountains a second time, the guide stated by signs that this was only a spur of the Rocky Mountains. After traveling some distance we found the trail which was very bad and very difficult to follow. Traveled about ten miles. Weather cold and cloudy. Feed scarce. Snowed during the night.

THURSDAY, NOVEMBER 25, 1858. The guide, in spite of coaxing, offers, and even threats of stripping him of all he had, left us. We were now in anything but a pleasant predicament. Here we were in a valley, surrounded by mountains covered with vast depth of snow, with a track that we were liable to lose the next minute. We held a council and determined to proceed. We traveled but a short distance and by good fortune kept the track all day. John Schaeffter lost his fine pony. Could not be found. We strongly suspicion that the guide has stolen her. Weather cold and snowy.

FRIDAY, NOVEMBER 26, 1858. Lost the trail soon after starting. It was vain to look for it. We determined to ascend the mountain ahead of us. In our passage up we saw several blazes in all directions; and here and there we saw trees rubbed close to the snow as though done by pack animals. These signs were cheering; and we went to work with a will in shoveling and beating out a track. About four in the afternoon we arrived within about a quarter of a mile of the summit. Jim Smith, Houck, and Amesbury went on ahead to see what were the prospects for a descent. After spending some time they came to us; and we proceeded. The sun was nearly down when we gained the summit.

Never shall I forget the mingled emotions I experienced, as the magnificent but to us heart-sickening prospect burst upon our view. The snow on the summit was so deep that good sized pine trees resembled brush and their tops resembling huge boulders of marble; while in every direction far as the eye could reach, nothing was to be seen but snow-capped mountains with their interesting valleys meandering in every direction. The only slightest hope that was held out to us was a river, far, far below. This we all agreed must run out of the mountains on the western side; and it might eventually lead us to an Indian camp. Two or three had started down to make a track; and we had to wait till they signaled us to come down. It was intensely cold. In spite of our exertions to keep warm, we were approaching that drowsy state, a sure forerunner of death by freezing. At last the welcome signal was given.

It was a solemn moment and one that will never be obliterated from my memory as our little band of ten stood on the snow-crowned summit on that bitter cold November evening. We had but little time for reflection, for the shades of night was approaching rapidly. No fuel was to be had, and we knew that; did we spend that night on the mountain, the ensuing morning would, in all human probability, find but few, if any, left to tell the sad tale of the pioneer party from Minnesota. The only alternative was to abandon our animals and, retracing our steps with what speed we might, endeavor to regain the plains on the east side of the mountains, where at least there was game and we might possibly winter[15]—or to push

[15] They feared the horses could not have survived the retreat and they believed spending the winter among the Blackfoot was a too dangerous prospect. *Faribault Central Republican,* 6 July 1859.

boldly on in the hope that the valley below us was the one leading us out of the mountains to the Kootenay Fort.

The latter course involved a terrible risk. We had only six days' provisions left, and, should our hypothesis prove incorrect and no trail found in the valley below, it was almost certain that every one of us would perish by cold and hunger, as, unless some other route could be found, it would be impossible for us to retrace our steps. Taking these into consideration we held a council, and all was unanimous for going ahead. Had a single voice been heard in favor of returning, we had never crossed the mountains; but perilous as was our position, not one of the little band faltered. "Onward" had ever been our motto and was so still. And without further hesitation we commenced the descent.

We had not proceeded but a short distance before the mountain became so steep that neither man nor horse could retain their footing for the distance of about five hundred feet. As soon as we gained footing we divested the animals of their packs and shoved them one by one over the ridge; and for the first few hundred feet they rolled down headlong. Out of fourteen animals, twelve reached *comparatively* level ground in safety, two being killed by the fall. At one time I thought I should lose my horse, as he got completely wedged between two trees. We hastened to his assistance; and, while cutting the tree, he gave a tremendous effort and released himself. We continued the descent till we came to the edge of a precipice several hundred feet in depth which arrested our progress.

It was now quite dark, and we camped on a ledge of rocks where the snow was not very deep. With considerable difficulty we succeeded in keeping up a fire through the night. As soon as we began to get warm, we discovered to our dismay that two or three of our party were slightly frozen. One young fellow, named Gibson, had his feet very badly frosted.

SATURDAY, NOVEMBER 27, 1858. Morning came at last. As soon as it was light enough to see our way, we gathered up the packs that were scattered in every direction. Our poor animals stood where we had left them. We now resumed our toilsome way down the mountain. Our descent was very difficult. In many places this morning horse and man lost their footing. At last reached the valley and level ground, having cut our way for some distance. About midday, to our great joy, we struck a broad, open trail—no snow—and though not loud but heartfelt and earnest was the prayer of thanksgiving that ascended from more than one breast. Through this valley runs Elk River, the river we saw from the summit.[16] Our animals are now failing rapidly. Traveled about six miles and camped for the benefit of our animals. Feed still scarce. Snow during the night.

SUNDAY, NOVEMBER 28, 1858. Traveled about eight miles. Trail good and plain. Weather clear and fine. Still skirting Elk River. No snow at night camp. Feed scarce, and no game except the trout in the river. Mountains on each side, and we are now on a piece of table land about one thousand feet above the river.

MONDAY, NOVEMBER 29, 1858. Traveled about eight miles. Followed Elk River and crossed it near its junction with the Kootenay River. Crossed Kootenay River just below the mouth of Elk. The Kootenay at the point of crossing is I should judge 200 feet wide, very clear, and rapid, and very deep in places. After ascending to the table land, which is at a considerable elevation from the bed of the river, we found a fresh horse track which was a good omen. Camped about two miles from the crossing. Had to carry water from the river. Feed for animals fair. Weather during the day clear and fine. Night had a slight snow. We are traveling slow in order to recruit our horses; and we are living now on very meager rations.

---

[16] The party reached the Elk River probably near present Elko, British Columbia. Spry, *The Palliser Expedition,* map 4.

TUESDAY, NOVEMBER 30, 1858. Crossed the Kootenay about three miles below last night's camp. River not so wide but deeper. As Jim Smith was sounding the depth of the river before crossing on horseback, the horse stopped where the water was at midside. Finding that coaxing had no effect, he had recourse to the cudgel, which he laid on pretty heavy. By *some means*, the horse and him parted company. Jim, however, got ashore in a very indignant mood. The banks on the river are very steep. Character of the country on the table lands chiefly yellow pine openings with very poor soil. There are few clear spots of prairie here and there. The valley here, from mountains to mountains, is of considerable width but does not hold forth any agricultural inducements. It is very picturesque but almost destitute of water. Passed two small lakes.

I do not agree with the [Jesuit missionary] Rev. Father [Pierre] De Smet's account of this country as published some years ago in the *Missouri Republican* where he extols the soil and stating that the proportions of prairie and timber were about equal.[17] It is true that there are few spots where the land could be cultivated with advantage with such produce as could stand the rigorous seasons of latitude 49° 30″ North; but those spots are scarce and far between. Weather cold. Feed good. Traveled about ten miles and camped near a small lake.

WEDNESDAY, DECEMBER 1, 1858. This morning we met some Kutenai Indians,[18] from whom we learned that we were drawing near to the fort. After traveling about ten miles,

---

[17] *Dictionary of Canadian Biography,* s.v. "De Smet, Pierre-Jean," by William L. Davis.

[18] The Kutenai Indians were located in the Kootenay River region and extended into Montana and Idaho. Swanton, *Indian Tribes of North America,* pp. 392–393, 575.

Concerning the Kootenai and Kootenay spellings for various geographic features: the former is generally American usage and the latter Canadian usage. The Kutenai spelling for the Indians is still another variation.

we finally reached the trading post[19] under charge of Mr. Linklater, a native of one of the Orkney Islands. This post is nothing but a poor log shanty with no means of defense whatever. It is situated on an open flat with plenty of wood and water near at hand. Around the fort we saw quite a number of Indian lodges, some made of skin but the majority were made of rushes woven together. There is besides the post three or four log buildings, the largest being used for house of worship as these Kutenai profess to be very pious, their faith being Roman Catholicism.

As we had encountered but little snow from our exit out the pass to this place, we naturally inferred that we could proceed to Colville very well. The Master, Mr. Linklater, informed us that we had better make tracks as quick as possible, that it was no uncommon thing for it to snow to the depth of four feet between that place and Colville. Comparatively no snow falling at the base of the Rocky Mountains. He also informed us that considerable danger was apprehended from the Spokans, Pen d'Oreilles, Nez Perce, and Okanagons or Colville Indians,[20] as they had been at war with the Americans during last summer. This was a dampener upon our feelings; but as we had run the gauntlet through the Blackfoot country on the east side of the mountains, we concluded to run the same risks on this side.

[19] The trading post on the Tobacco Plains, a few miles south of the international border. *Chatfield Democrat,* 18, 25 June 1859; *St. Paul Daily Pioneer and Democrat,* 25 June 1859; *Faribault Central Republican,* 22 June 1859; *Mankato Weekly Independent,* 16 July 1859.

There is no Kootenay trading post journal for this date in the Hudson's Bay Company Archives, Provincial Archives of Manitoba. Judith Hudson Beattie to author, August 19, 1987.

[20] The Spokan and Pen d'Oreille were related tribes. The Pen d'Oreille were so designated by Europeans because they wore large shell earrings. They called themselves Kalispel, said to mean camas. Nez Perce is a French appellation signifying pierced noses. Okanagon is derived from the river of the same name. The Colville were named after Fort Colville, the Hudson's Bay Post. Swanton, *Indian Tribes of North America,* pp. 399–403, 421–422, 430–433, 444–445.

We now commenced to trade with the Indians our useless trinkets and worn out clothing for provisions in which we had the best of the trade. We laid in a supply of provisions for seventeen days, being the time that Mr. Linklater said it would take us. Hall traded off his horse and got a good one in return. When the vesper hour was tolled at eve by a small bell, the Indians suddenly left our camp and made for the chapel, old and young, to perform the evening service. The service lasted I should think about fifteen minutes; and as the day was bitter cold and no fire in the chapel, they must have suffered somewhat from the cold. They appear to be very zealous and devout in the performance of their rites. They are strictly honest; and you can lay anything down and leave it without any fears of it being stolen. If any of them is tempted to steal it, all you have to do is to inform the chief that some of his men have stolen such an article and it will be forthcoming in a few minutes.

We were presented with a fine mess of dried buffalo meat and about a pound of fresh butter by the chief, O-kak-kik-ha-lo-la, the latter article made by his family. It was very creditable butter and far superior to the rancid trash that is set on the tables of many of the western hotels. These Indians have about forty head of cattle and all in fine order. I presume that they procured them from the Colville settlement. They are highly prized by them and will not part with one for any consideration. They also cultivate small patches of wheat and potatoes. The latter article is not to be depended upon, as they are subject to heavy frost every month in the year.

This tribe of Indians is small, numbering in all about five hundred souls. They were once a large and powerful tribe; but continual hostilities with the neighboring tribes have reduced them to their present low state. They are at peace with all the Indians on the west side; but in the summer seasons when they cross the mountains to lay in a winter supply of buffalo meat, they are constantly harassed by the Blackfeet. They have large bands of fine horses; but during the winter season the dogs are put in requisition as beast of burden.

At night we visited several of the lodges; and at each one we were invited to partake of some refreshments. About nine o'clock prayers were said in each lodge at the tinkling of a cow bell, which could be distinctly heard all over the camp, by the head man of each family. After prayers we retired to our own quarters. Night bitter cold.

THURSDAY, DECEMBER 2, 1858.   Stayed in camp all day preparing for our trip, also procured a chart of the route from Mr. Linklater. Traded considerably with the Indians. Visited their lodges at night. They were very clamorous for salt and soap. These two articles command a good trade among these Indians. We parted with all we could spare; but they were not satisfied. They wanted all, which we positively refused to do. Day and night extremely cold.

CHAPTER 5

The Grim Reality of Winter Survival: Kootenay Trading Post to Winter Camp

[After two days at the Kootenay post, they pushed on. The seasoned travelers were not prepared mentally nor by experience for what was ahead, but they plunged on with determination. Following the Kootenai River for two weeks, on its U-shaped dip into Montana and Idaho and back into British Columbia, they came to Duck Lake in the lower reaches of Kootenay Lake through which the river passed, in mid-December.

After resting for a day at a small Kutenai Indian encampment, they pushed southward and upward. Into increasing snow depths and difficulties for the horses, the party thought it prudent to change their immediate objective. Four men continued on snowshoes headed for the Colville Valley, and Jones with four others returned with their horses to the Duck Lake Indian encampment.

Here, about a mile from the Indians, they erected a temporary "lodge in the usual conical shape and covered it with boughs" and a more permanent eight by twelve log shanty. The Kutenai were Catholic converts and the Minnesotans were welcome guests at their Christmas and New Years ceremonies and feasts.

The grim reality of their circumstances soon set in. Their subsistence was reduced to a litany of moss, minnows, and "a few garlics," enhanced by occasional meat as their horses began to die. The Indians were not much better off except that this was apparently a normal situation for them in the dead of winter. Weeks later, faced with a finite quantity of potential horse meat that would not be sufficient for the five men until "the snow went off," Jones and two others decided to strike out on snowshoes for Colville.]

* * *

FRIDAY, DECEMBER 3, 1858. Bid farewell to Linklater and young Gibson, whom we were compelled to leave behind in charge of Mr. Linklater as his feet were so badly frozen as to preclude all possibility of travel.[1] Shook hands with the Indians and started. As the afternoon was considerably advanced, we only gained five miles. Crossed two running streams. Skirting the river.[2] Camped on a small spot of prairie near the banks of the river. Feed plenty. Weather very cold with snow at night.

SATURDAY, DECEMBER 4, 1858. Traveled about fifteen miles. Trail very rough and rocky. Still skirting the river. Feed scarce. Mountains on each side of us. Valley very narrow. Weather extremely cold.

SUNDAY, DECEMBER 5, 1858. Traveled about fifteen miles. Trail very rough and feed for animals very scarce. Our mule gave out; and we had to leave her. She had evidently received some internal injury in our descent from the last mountain as from that time she rapidly failed. We regretted her loss very much as she was quite a favorite.

[1] Gibson continued on the journey in the spring and arrived at The Dalles with Jim Smith and Schaeffter, 8 June. See note 13 below.

[2] The trail was following the Kootenai River which crosses the extreme northwest corner of Montana, the northeast corner of the Idaho panhandle, and back into British Columbia.

The topographic maps 1:500 000 of the United States Geological Survey for Montana and Idaho and that of the Canada, Department of Energy, Mines, and Resources for Okanagan-Kootenay give helpful orientation for this part of the trek.

MONDAY, DECEMBER 6, 1858. Traveled about ten miles. Trail very rough. Weather bitter cold. Found the river froze over this morning at a point. It is still open in many places. An Indian came into camp and stayed with us all night. Feed better but still scarce.

TUESDAY, DECEMBER 7, 1858. Traveled about three miles and came to a small Indian camp. The Indians advised us to camp and wait for the river to freeze so that we might cross, as it would certainly freeze over before morning. So we camped. These Indians were very poor and destitute, subsisting entirely on fish. Weather very cold. Feed better.

WEDNESDAY, DECEMBER 8, 1858. The river still open; and as we had not come to the regular crossing we concluded that we would start. After traveling about ten miles, we came to the crossing where there was a large encampment of Indians. The river was open; and we camped on its banks. Some hunters returned in the afternoon with a black-tailed deer they had killed through the assistance of our dog. We procured a supply which was relished exceedingly. The lodges were all made of rushes. The chief of this band was laid up with a broken leg. Weather very cold. Snow fell during the night.

THURSDAY, DECEMBER 9, 1858. This morning we found the river closed, the ice being about two and a half inches thick. We went to work and piled snow clear across and poured water over it, so that in about half an hour afterwards we crossed one at the time with ease against the expostulation and much to the astonishment of the Indians. They set us down as perfect daredevils. Traveled about six miles. Trail rough. Still following the river. Weather cold and snowing. Saw a duck nearly white in an open spot of the river.

FRIDAY, DECEMBER 10, 1858. Traveled about fifteen miles. Trail very rough. Weather mild and snowing. Feed plenty.

SATURDAY, DECEMBER 11, 1858. Traveled about sixteen miles. Trail still very rough and brushy. Ascended a small mountain which was very steep and rocky. In descending, our path lay close to a precipice, on the border of which a flimsy barricade had been erected; the path was so narrow that I momentarily expected that some of our animals would go over, and as good luck would favor us we arrived at its base in safety. Weather mild and snowing. Feed scarce.

SUNDAY, DECEMBER 12, 1858. Traveled about fifteen miles. Trail fair. Passed an Indian camp in the morning, creating much astonishment among the natives. We enquired whether we were on the road to Klap-keake (fort) and received an affirmative answer. Camped on the banks of Milaine River.[3] This stream is about sixty feet wide, shallow but very rapid with rocky bottom. Weather mild and snowing. Feed scarce.

MONDAY, DECEMBER 13, 1858. Traveled about ten miles. Our trail led over a mountainous district bordering the river. Amesbury's horse gave out and had to leave him. Saw a deer and plenty of wolf tracks. Snowed all day and night. The snow is now about a foot deep. Feed very scarce.

TUESDAY, DECEMBER 14, 1858. My horse couldn't be found this morning. Jim and myself stayed till noon looking for him. Our search proving unavailing, we concluded to leave him as time was precious. Arrived at camp about 9 P.M. It was very dark when we arrived; and it was with much difficulty we could keep the trail which was very rough and hilly. Our camp lay on the banks of Flat River.[4] Feed excellent in the valley. Snowed all day and night. Traveled about fifteen miles.

WEDNESDAY, DECEMBER 15, 1858. Stayed in camp to give our animals rest and feed, as they are failing fast. Houck and

[3] This is probably Moyie River which empties into the Kootenai River at present Moyie Springs, Idaho.

[4] This is probably Goat River which enters the Kootenay near present Creston, British Columbia.

Amesbury returned to look for the missing animals. They were fortunate in finding mine; but Amesbury's was unable to travel. Experienced during the twenty-four hours thaw, rain, and snow.

THURSDAY, DECEMBER 16, 1858.   Traveled about ten miles over a rough trail and arrived at Duck Lakes, or the second crossing of the Kootenay River from the post.[5] Here we found an encampment of about [a] dozen rush lodges.[6] These Kutenai we also found to be religious and friendly but much poorer in worldly goods than those at the fort. We were now about out of provisions. Saw two white geese flying southward. Feed scarce. Weather mild and thawing. Camped about a quarter of a mile from their camp.

FRIDAY, DECEMBER 17, 1858.   Stayed in camp. Houck and Amesbury returned this morning. Traded some ammunition with the Indian for dried fish and about a quart of wheat. Weather mild and raining. Slept for the first time under cover since leaving Fort Garry, having slept in the chief's lodge.

SATURDAY, DECEMBER 18, 1858.   Traded my horse for a fresh one. Crossed the river on the ice. Passed through a marsh about five miles in width. Ascended a mountain and camped on its summit. Traveled about eight miles.[7] Weather mild and cloudy during the day. Rained hard all night.

---

[5]   Duck Lake is the southern extremity of Flatbow Lake, presently designated Kootenay Lake, a part of the Kootenay River.

[6]   In their report to the *Faribault Central Republican,* 6 July 1859, Jones and Houck specified there were eight lodges at this encampment.

[7]   These entries do not give enough information to trace the route they were attempting to follow. As will be noted in successive entries, they retraced their steps to Duck Lake to camp for the winter. In late February, they set out again along the same route and succeeded, arriving at Pend Oreille Lake in early March. From the distance between these two points and the travel time involved, the route they were following was generally southward, with possibly the last long leg along the Pack River.

SUNDAY, DECEMBER 19, 1858. Descended the mountain and traveled through a valley. Passed three small lakes. Trail very bad. We find that the farther we advance the deeper the snow is getting. Crossed several small creeks. No feed for animals. Our buffalo meat all gone. Made about 12 miles. Weather rained hard all day. Clear at night.

MONDAY, DECEMBER 20, 1858. Had considerable trouble in finding our horses. They had wandered a considerable distance in search of food. Traveled about three miles; and the snow is now at an average depth of three feet. Camped in a cedar bottom.

The increasing depth of snow warned us that we must either abandon our stock or make up our minds to winter at Duck Lakes on the Kootenay River, where we were told by Mr. Linklater that stock wintered well. We held a consultation, and finally determined that four of the party should go on to Colville on snowshoes, and the remaining five return to Duck Lakes and endeavor to winter there.[8]

What a fearful night we spent. Heavy snow accompanied with terrible winds. Huge trees falling all around us. The darkness was appalling. Every moment we expected to be crushed by the falling timber. We lay there in our blankets in mute resignation, almost wishing at times that some friendly tree would fall and end our sufferings.

The lot fell upon Messrs. Hall, Amesbury, Emehiser, and Hodgeson, to make the best of their way to Colville. I shall revert to their trials and sufferings hereafter.

TUESDAY, DECEMBER 21, 1858. Upon examination we found that none of the horses or any of the party had suffered any bodily injuries from the terrible storm of last night. Houck, Jones, Smith, Palmer, and Schaeffter composed the company who were to return. We bid a sad farewell to the boys

---

[8] One of the considerations was that it would be impossible to go any further with the horses. *Faribault Central Republican*, 6 July 1859.

and started with heavy hearts. Little did we expect on that eventful morning that we should ever see each other again. One party had a trackless forest for a long distance and with a scanty supply of provision. The other to return without provisions and depend on the Indians for a livelihood, or if that was refused, to eat our horses.

WEDNESDAY, DECEMBER 22, 1858.   Camped at the lake we passed on Sunday. Weather cold and freezing during the day. Night clear and cold.

THURSDAY, DECEMBER 23, 1858.   Arrived at Duck Lakes at dusk. The Indians were surprised to see us; or else they feigned it. We made known to them that we intended to camp there till the snow went off. Our poor animals had nothing to eat since leaving this place. We now turned them out in a feeble state to shift for themselves. We put our traps in the chief's lodge; and for the present we made it our quarters.

FRIDAY, DECEMBER 24, 1858.   Occupied the day in building a temporary lodge about a mile from the Indian encampment, at the foot of the mountains. We made our lodge in the usual conical shape and covered it with pine boughs.

Having returned to the Indian camp we found them making preparations to celebrate Christmas. A little curious how they should know it to be Christmas, we by signs enquired how they kept the knowledge of the months and days. From signs we learned that a missionary priest always pays them a visit during the summer or fall; and when he comes he gives them a piece of paper marked with the days of the week as well as the month. The Indian is then told what day it is and to perforate a hole upon each day. Christmas was marked upon the paper in the shape of a cross and New Years with a peculiar mark. They showed us the paper and pointed out the day we first came with a perforation for each man in the company, and also noted the day we returned with five perforations opposite.

Receiving an invitation to participate in their festivities, we nodded our head with gratified assent. The festivities commenced by a *Cicero* rushing frantically in a seminudity state from the lodge into the open air and commenced *spouting* in good earnest. His auditors evidently not appreciating his gesture or oratory were huddled together around the fire in their respective lodges. The chill air seemed to have a wonderful effect on him at times, for he would abruptly cease while in the *zenith* of his *eloquence* and hasten to the fire to feel its genial warmth. He would go out at intervals of every fifteen minutes and harangue an audience that was not visible until the cold drove him in again. In this manner he kept speaking till

"Night, drew her sable mantle around,
And pinned it with a star."

Not understanding the tenor of his speech, we manifested our indifference by quietly ensconcing ourselves in an unoccupied corner of the lodge and solaced ourselves with smoking the weed.

About eight o'clock P.M., we should judge, the inmates of the lodges were called together by a violent ringing of a cowbell. Having all assembled in the chief's lodge, (the one we were in) prayers were said and hymns sang in a compound mixture of French, Latin, and Indian, taught to them by the priest. After prayers they retired to their respective lodges; a few minutes after, the squaws came in, in single file, and deposited their contributions of smoked venison and Mis-as-qui-tom-i-ca or service berries at the foot of the altar. The altar was formed out of a square box made from cedar bark. The box was covered with a mat of rushes and at the foot was also a mat. Catholic pictures were pinned to the side of the lodge over the altar. Each squaw upon depositing her contribution would cross herself in a pious manner before the altar and receive a *benedictive* from the chief who is acting priest for the band. These contributions were for the coming feast on the morrow.

Upon the completion of the donations, the venison was put

into a large kettle and the berries in another, and boiled till they were thoroughly cooked. While the process of cooking was going on, the Indians wiled the passing hours till the dawn of the morning with talking and smoking. Not being interested in their conversation, we sought the sweet influence of balmy slumber.

SATURDAY, DECEMBER 25, 1858. At the early tint of morn we were aroused by that villainous cowbell and admonished that it was time for prayers. The Indians, both great and small, old and young, having been assembled, prayers were said and hymns sang as usual. After prayers we became all seated; and the sacrament (so we inferred) was administered, in this manner: The priest's attendant filling a cup with the liquor of the berries, and a small piece of venison, giving it to the acting priest who pronounced a blessing and having partook passed it to the attendant, who in turn passed to each one present that had arrived at the years of discretion.

After the sacrament was administered, the squaws and children, who had been dressed in their *best style,* took their departure, the males remaining and seating themselves in a circle. Each one now armed himself with a large pan, kettle, or basket capable of containing fluid (the squaws make baskets capable of holding from a pint to several gallons without leaking, without the aid of pitch, tar, or any such substance) and we were told to do so likewise. An Indian now stepped forward and distributed the venison and berries, reserving for the priest and ourselves the largest and choicest portions. After eating a few moments, smoking and chatting was the order. Our pipes becoming empty, we all arose and started for the nearest wigwam where the same ceremony was repeated with the exception of prayers; and in like manner we visited every lodge. As soon as we issued out of one the squaws and children were ready to enter and feast upon what remained. After surfeiting ourselves to repletion, we finally finished the festive scene at noon, each of us carrying a large panful to the chief's tent. We had enough to last for three days.

SUNDAY, DECEMBER 26, 1858.   Removed to our temporary lodge. Snowed nearly all day. Clear at night.

MONDAY, DECEMBER 27, 1858.   Traded a gun and our dog for some fish, with the chief. We were to receive for the dog twenty day's supply of fresh fish. Which trade he never fulfilled. Occupied most of the day in cutting logs for our shanty. Snowed during the day and night.

TUESDAY, DECEMBER 28, 1858.   Raised the shanty. Weather clear and mild. Living now on fish.

WEDNESDAY, DECEMBER 29, 1858.   Occupied ourselves by working on the shanty. Weather clear and mild.

THURSDAY, DECEMBER 30, 1858.   Finished covering our shanty with pine boughs and chinking it with the same material. We had a piece of canvas to cover the opening of the doorway. Shanty—eight by twelve. For a *carpet,* we again had recourse to pine boughs. Snowed during the day and night. Moved into our shanty.

FRIDAY, DECEMBER 31, 1858.   Snowed all day and night. Received an invitation from the chief in the evening to participate in their New Year's Festival, which we gladly accepted and accompanied our cicerone to the camp. Prayers were said and donations given as at Christmas Eve.

SATURDAY, JANUARY 1, 1859.   At the close of the morning devotions the Indians armed themselves with guns, and forming themselves in a row outside fired an irregular volley, and repeating it for some minutes. We were then brought inside and formed into a row, the chief or priest standing at the head. At a signal being given the males marched in in single file, and as they entered shook us by the hands, and saluted us with "Ka-so-ke-u-ka," which means as near as we could learn, "Happy New Year." As they shook hands, they also fell into line. When the males were all in, and had shaken hands, and had formed themselves in a circle, the signal was given for the squaws and children to enter, when they saluted us in like manner. None escaped, even the tiny hand of the infant at the breast was grasped by all.

This part of the ceremony being ended, mass was performed, after which the sacrament was administered, upon the completion of which the squaws and children retired. The rest of the ceremony was similar with that of Christmas, with the exception that the headman of each lodge upon our entry made an exhortation, fired off a gun through the opening of the lodge above, prior to eating. The feast lasted till about one o'clock; and as soon as we were through, the chief with signs unmistakable informed us that we might *vamose;* not caring to argue the point with him we incontinently left for our own quarters, carrying with us a large panful of venison and berries.

It is little thought among civilized people that these holidays are observed by Indians who hardly ever see a white man but their own missionary; but such is the fact; and it is rigidly observed by all Indians on the Pacific Coast who have been converted to the Roman faith. These Indians place a high estimation upon their religion and attend to their devotions both morning and evening with great punctuality. One of our party, John Schaeffter, who is a Catholic, had a prayer book illustrated. He showed it to the Indians. They immediately recognized the halo or corona encircling the heads of the saints. They piously pointed to the heavens and crossed themselves. Showing them some daguerreotypes, they inquired if they were saints. Being replied in the negative they examined it with considerable curiosity, especially the portraits of the "loved ones" who displayed crinoline to *advantage.*[9]

SUNDAY, JANUARY 2, 1859.   Clear and mild during the day. Rained during the day.

---

[9] The account of the Christmas and New Years experience appeared in ibid.; *Chatfield Democrat,* 23 July 1859.

MONDAY, JANUARY 3, 1859. Snowed hard all morning. Thawed in the afternoon and clear at night.

TUESDAY, JANUARY 4, 1859. Clear and cold both day and night. Indians brought up a few dried fish for which we traded.[10]

WEDNESDAY, JANUARY 5, 1859. Clear and cold. Night same. Indians brought some minnows which they caught in a net. Cooked them whole and eat them bones, fins, and all.

THURSDAY, JANUARY 6, 1859. Clear and cold. Night cold and cloudy. Traded for minnows as usual.

FRIDAY, JANUARY 7, 1859. Clear and cold. Night extremely so. Indians informed us that it would be seventy days before we could start. Traded for minnows, giving them old shirts and ammunition.

SATURDAY, JANUARY 8, 1859. No change in the weather. Procured the usual supply of minnows.

SUNDAY, JANUARY 9, 1859. No change in the weather. The last mess of pork and flour which we rationed down to one meal per week is gone as also our sugar and tea.

MONDAY, JANUARY 10, 1859. Clear and somewhat milder. Night cloudy. We are troubled with costiveness and suffer considerable pains from eating the minnows whole.

TUESDAY, JANUARY 11, 1859. Snowing both day and night. Procured some minnows as usual, also some moss which was cooked.

WEDNESDAY, JANUARY 12, 1859. Cloudy with snow squalls throughout the day and night. We are all complaining of being sick and very weak. Voiding blood.

---

[10] The accepted rate of exchange was "about 15 buckshot and three charges of powder for a mess" of small dried minnows. *Faribault Central Republican*, 6 July 1859.

THURSDAY, JANUARY 13, 1859. Clear and cold. Night cloudy but not so cold. Procured some minnows and moss as usual.

FRIDAY, JANUARY 14, 1859.   Heavy snow all day. Warm and thawing during the night. The snow is now about three feet deep.

SATURDAY, JANUARY 15, 1859.   Clear and mild. Visited the Indian camp and found but three lodges left. Looked for our horses and found them all but one. We still complain of weakness.

SUNDAY, JANUARY 16, 1859.   Mild and clear. Thaw and snow at night. Procured some minnows and moss from the Indians. They will not permit us to fish.

MONDAY, JANUARY 17, 1859.   Warm and cloudy during day and night.

TUESDAY, JANUARY 18, 1859.   Warm and cloudy. Snow squalls during the night. Minnows and moss as usual.

WEDNESDAY, JANUARY 19, 1859.   Clear and mild. Freezing through the night.

THURSDAY, JANUARY 20, 1859.   Mild and clear with heavy winds during day and night. Minnows and moss as usual.

FRIDAY, JANUARY 21, 1859.   Mild and clear during day and night.

SATURDAY, JANUARY 22, 1859.   Mild and clear during the day. Cold and foggy through the night. Minnows, moss, and a few garlics.

SUNDAY, JANUARY 23, 1859.   Mild and cloudy. Cold at night.

MONDAY, JANUARY 24, 1859.   No change in the weather. Scraped the moldy flour from our flour sacks, and procured enough to make a *slapjack,* which we divided equally. It tasted very good. Minnows and moss as usual from the Indians.

TUESDAY, JANUARY 25, 1859.   Cold and cloudy during the day. Clear at night.

WEDNESDAY, JANUARY 26, 1859.   No change in the weather. Minnows and moss. Still becoming weaker and all despondent. We are continually talking of home, and what we should order at the restaurants. Houck says he would call for a good mess of "pork and beans." Jim Smith a mallard, lobster sauce, and a bottle of "Cabinet." Palmer roast beef and plum pudding; Dutch John corn beef, sauerkraut, and *Sweitzer Kase,* and several *gallons* of lager. As for myself, I have a hankering for a huge loaf of homemade bread and enough golden syrup to devour it with and to wash it down with sundry bottles of Edinburgh Ale.

THURSDAY, JANUARY 27, 1859.   No change in the weather till night when it cleared off and turned very cold. Minnows and moss.

FRIDAY, JANUARY 28, 1859.   No change.

SATURDAY, JANUARY 29, 1859.   Mild during the day. Cloudy and thawing during the night. Minnows and moss as usual.

SUNDAY, JANUARY 30, 1859.   No change. Went out and cut down some trees to procure moss. Took it to the Indians who prepared it.

MONDAY, JANUARY 31, 1859.   Mild and snowing during day and night. The Indians do not come to us regularly now. When we get out we have to take some ammunition and procure some.

TUESDAY, FEBRUARY 1, 1859.   Clear and thawing. Indians brought up some large fish which have just run up. Palmer calls them Tom cod.[11] Their liver is exactly like a cod. We found these fish quite a relief from the minnows. We took the roe out and made a sort of soup, seasoning it with few garlics which we had procured from the Indians. Stripped the entrails and boiled them with the fish.

WEDNESDAY, FEBRUARY 2, 1859.   Mild and snowing. Procured some moss and had it prepared by the Indians.

THURSDAY, FEBRUARY 3, 1859.   Warm and thawing. Tom cods. We are commencing to recruit.

FRIDAY, FEBRUARY 4, 1859.   Warm and thawing. Heavy snow fell during the night. The snow is now four feet on a level.

SATURDAY, FEBRUARY 5, 1859.   Mild and snowing. Two Indians came into camp this morning from the Kootenay trading post. We recognized them; and they appeared to be glad to see us. They are couriers sent from that post to Colville with the Hudson's Bay mail, for which service they get "thirty-six skins" which is equivalent to about $18.00 of American money. The trip is usually performed in about three weeks, including stoppages. We wrote a letter to Amesbury begging for tobacco. We would much prefer flour, etc., but the couriers could not pack it as they were traveling on snowshoes. They promised to return in nine "sleeps" or nine days. They stayed with us all night. We thought some of accompanying them; but in our present weak state we knew that we were not able to keep up with them; so we desisted.

SUNDAY, FEBRUARY 6, 1859.   Snow squalls through the day. Houck and myself procured snowshoes and looked for the horses. We found them all but one. Tom cod and moss as usual.

MONDAY, FEBRUARY 7, 1859.   Clear and cold.

[11] "They appear to be a cross between the cod and eel." Ibid.

TUESDAY, FEBRUARY 8, 1859.   Clear and cold. Snow during the night. Wolves howled all around our shanty.

WEDNESDAY, FEBRUARY 9, 1859.   Cold and cloudy during the day and night.

THURSDAY, FEBRUARY 10, 1859.   No change in the weather. Tom cods getting scarce.

FRIDAY, FEBRUARY 11, 1859.   Cool and clear during day and night.

SATURDAY, FEBRUARY 12, 1859.   We were waked up this morning by an Indian lad who imparted the unwelcome intelligence that my horse was dead. I hardly credited it, for I had seen him two or three days before in very good order. He assured us it was the fact. Houck and myself accompanied the lad; and we found sure enough that he was dead, having died of eating snake grass which was frozen and full of ice creating a cold. The crows had already been at work. We skinned him and gave the Indians one half of the carcass including the entrails. The other we took home, dried a portion, and feasted ourselves on the balance. The heart and liver we found to be covered with large black spots; but that did not deter us from devouring it. Long privations and hunger made it seem as a delicacy and we relished it accordingly. This, to persons who have not suffered as we have, may seem a horrid diet; but to us it was a banquet.

SUNDAY, FEBRUARY 13, 1859.   Clear and warm. Thawing at night.

MONDAY, FEBRUARY 14, 1859.   St. Valentine's Day. The thought naturally brought to our minds the *Valentines* we left behind us and conversed freely and unreservedly of the past and our prospects for the future. Weather mild and thawing during day and night.

TUESDAY, FEBRUARY 15, 1859.   No change in the weather. Hearing that Amesbury's horse was about to give up the ghost from the same disease of which mine had died, we drove him up to our camp which was but a short distance and knocked him in the head. Gave the Indians the entrails and a portion of the hide. We kept the balance ourselves. Smoked about half of him for future use. The bones we made soup of. Wolves and coyotes howled all around us when darkness set in; and some came very near the cabin. There was nothing left of the horse where we slaughtered him but the offal; and having the meat in the shanty the scent naturally attracted them hither.

WEDNESDAY, FEBRUARY 16, 1859.   Clear and cold during day and night.

THURSDAY, FEBRUARY 17, 1859.   Mild and snowing throughout day and night.

FRIDAY, FEBRUARY 18, 1859.   No change in the weather.

SATURDAY, FEBRUARY 19, 1859.   No change in the weather.

SUNDAY, FEBRUARY 20, 1859.   No change. Anxiously awaiting the arrival of the couriers, as they are overdue.

MONDAY, FEBRUARY 21, 1859.   No change.

TUESDAY, FEBRUARY 22, 1859.   No change.[12]

WEDNESDAY, FEBRUARY 23, 1859.   Mild with heavy snow. The messengers have not arrived. Held a consultation at night and came to conclusion that three of us should try and make our [way] to Colville. The reason for this is, that at the rate we were eating our horse meat, we would not have enough to last us, reckoning those that were still

[12] They killed another horse to replenish their larder. Ibid.

living, till the snow went off. It fell upon the lot of Houck, Jones, and Palmer to go.[13]

---

[13] Jim Smith and Schaeffter remained behind. The snow was heavy, most of the Indians departed, and they subsisted mostly on moss and the inner bark of pine trees. They left their winter quarters with Gibson on 29 April, and with some difficulty arrived at The Dalles, 8 June. *The Dalles Journal,* undated, copied by Jones at the end of his journal; see note 1 above.

For reasons not stated, there was concern about the arrival of Smith in the gold country. A notice appeared in each tri-weekly issue of a Victoria newspaper for a month commencing 29 March 1859: "INFORMATION Wanted of James E. Smith, Jun'r. (one of a party of nine) who left St. Paul, Minnesota, for Fraser River, *via* the Selkirk Settlements and Edmonton House, in July 1858. Any particulars as to the whereabouts of the above named party, would be thankfully received by SOUTHGATE & MITCHELL, Victoria." Southgate and Mitchell were commission merchants in Victoria, British Columbia, and San Francisco. *Victoria Gazette,* 9 April, 7 May 1859.

Faltering Persistence Prevails:
Winter Camp to The Dalles

[Calculating that there was only sufficient horse flesh to sustain two men until the winter snows abated, the Minnesotans decided to divide again. Jones and two others got snowshoes from the Indians and set out for the Colville Valley. Retracing their previous steps, they moved southward and reached Pend Oreille Lake in northern Idaho in a week.

Some friendly Indians treated them to a welcome boiled venison-coon-muskrat dinner with a side dish of "very dirty venison tallow." A few miles down the Pend Oreille River, other Indians gave them news of the four members of their party that had pushed on in December rather than to winter at Duck Lake.

In some respects, the most difficult experience was still ahead. They had to cross a mountain range to the westward before they reached the Colville Valley. At one point, weakened by heavy snow, cold temperatures, and bleeding feet, Jones gave up, resigned to freezing or starving to death. A companion finally coaxed and forced him to press on.

They found settlers in the Colville Valley and others of their party who had come on before. The quest for Fraser gold no longer bound the Minnesotans together and they now began to take advantage of promise or opportunity of employment wherever it might lead them. Jones recuperated for a month and then decided to join a party of four others bound for The Dalles.

They followed the Colville Road southward to Walla Walla and on to the Columbia River. From there, they traveled along the Oregon bank of the Columbia and reached their destination on April 29. Jones had left Faribault, Minnesota, nine months before with a different goal in mind.]

*   *   *

THURSDAY, FEBRUARY 24, 1859. Procured three pair of snowshoes from the Indians. At noon we made preparations to start, taking with us two blankets and ten pounds of dried horse meat apiece, calculating that it would take us about ten days to make the trip. The Indians said it was only five days.

While we were making preparations, three squaws made their appearance with a supply of moss which they wished to trade. We made known to them our intention of starting for the fort. They then knelt down and offered up prayers to the Giver of all Good for our welfare and a prosperous journey. That the prayers were said in the pure earnestness of their hearts I have not the least doubt, for I flatter myself that I am a tolerable judge of human nature. Upon rising they shook our hands, kissed us, and cried. At such a burst of warm-hearted feeling which I never once dreamed they possessed, I came near blubbering myself. They again knelt as we started. Though not understanding their language, we knew sufficient enough that they implored the Great Spirit to guide us through in safety and to shield us from all harm.

Stopped a few moments at the Indian camp where the squaws also prayed for us. As for the men, they appeared to be indifferent. Crossed the river and marsh and camped at the foot of the hill, distance five miles from winter quarters.

FRIDAY, FEBRUARY 25, 1859. Had considerable difficulty in ascending the hill with snowshoes, as it was very steep in places. Found the trail of the Indian couriers on top of the hill, followed it, and only made about six miles.

SATURDAY, FEBRUARY 26, 1859.   The trail was very dim and hardly perceptible. Many times through the day we lost it and as often found it. Weather mild and pleasant. Cut down pine branches to lay down on. Built a fire and slept very comfortable. Have no idea how far we traveled.

SUNDAY, FEBRUARY 27, 1859.   Lost the trail altogether soon after starting. We have now passed the spot where we turned back. The party of four that preceded us promised that they would blaze their way through, so that if it should happen we would be compelled to come through before the snow went off we would have a guide. We searched in vain the whole breadth of the valley for the blazes. They were evidently buried under the snow, as it was very deep. We are now traveling by random but still following the valley.

MONDAY, FEBRUARY 28, 1859.   No trail or blazes found. Had to go through some very heavy thickets. Early this morning we held a consultation as to whether we should undertake it. Now, I am a considerable believer in dreams; and last night I dreamed that we were on the right course, and that eventually we should find a trail. So that when the consultation was held, I was fully in favor of pushing forward; and Houck and Palmer finally acquiesced.

TUESDAY, MARCH 1, 1859.   Last night I dreamed that we found a snowshoe trail, which I imparted to my companions, expressing at the same time the certainty that we should. Traveled through very deep snow. About the middle of the afternoon sure enough, we did find one on a small river we were going to cross. The river was froze over. Followed the river and had good traveling. Today the strings of my snowshoes, in spite of all I could do to prevent it, cut into my toes and heels which bled freely.

WEDNESDAY, MARCH 2, 1859.   Last night I dreamed that we came to Flat Head Lake. The boys now call me the "Dreamer" and will not start till I have imparted my dream. Followed the trail and came to Flat Head, or Pend Oreille Lake,[1] late in the afternoon. Crossed a portion of it and camped on its banks. The eastern portion of the lake was open; we saw quite a number of swans, geese, and ducks. The scenery around this lake is sublime. My feet were very painful, the blood oozing out of my moccasins.

THURSDAY, MARCH 3, 1859.   According to the vision of last night I told the boys that they might eat a good meal of horse meat as we should come to an Indian camp some time during the day, which advice they would not take, it being prudent not to do so.

Followed the lake for some distance and saw an Indian in a canoe fishing. We made for him and soon had the satisfaction of knowing that a camp was nearby. He started to herald our approach. In about an hour we arrived at a large lodge, where I should judge three or four families were living. These Indians are Pen d'Oreilles; and though they were somewhat hostile to the Americans last summer, they received us with a warm welcome. We noticed a large pot full of meat on the fire. As soon as it was cooked the meat was placed in a basket and set before us. The contents of the basket proved to be venison, coon, and muskrat. Being very hungry, we went in with a will, making no distinction but took it as it came. The broth which was thickly covered with fat a shade darker than "charcoal," was scooped out with horn spoons. They also set us out some very dirty venison tallow to eat with our meat, which was very

---

[1] The party had probably been following Pack River to Pend Oreille Lake in the Idaho panhandle. See note 7, chapter 5, above.

This last leg of the journey can be traced reasonably well on the topographic maps 1:500 000 of Canada, Department of Energy, Mines, and Resources for Okanagan-Kootenay and the United States Geological Survey for Idaho and Washington.

much relished then by us. Having eat to repletion, we returned thanks to "old John," the chief, for his kindness. I procured a fresh pair of snowshoes for a trifling consideration. We also traded for some venison and coon meat.

Bidding them farewell, we now trudged our way along the banks of the Pend Oreille River, which is broad, shallow, and very sluggish stream for some distance; and in its present stage, which is very low, it has no perceptible current. Camped about five miles from the Indian lodge. The snow is not as deep in this valley. River open. Weather pleasant.

FRIDAY, MARCH 4, 1859.   Told the boys that we should see during the day an Indian and his squaw on the opposite side of the river, and that we should hear good news. Traveled over very rough banks this morning. At noon we descried two Indians on the opposite banks. Upon discovering us they came across in their canoe; and we reached their lodge about the same time. The Indian and his squaw welcomed us. The lodge was small. We here found three Indians and three squaws, two of them dressed in calico dresses and their hair done up *alamode* American, parted in the middle and tacked up behind. From them we learned about Hall and his party that preceded us. As near as we could learn from them, they must have went a very circuitous route and nearly starved. They showed us a number of things which we recognized as belonging to individuals of the party.

As it was snowing very hard, we concluded to stop all night with them. They were badly off for provisions depending entirely upon the "suckers" which they caught. They informed us that the river was open clear to the Columbia, with the exception of a quarter of a mile where we had to make a portage. We engaged the old man to take us to the Pen d'Oreille Mission, which is situated at the foot of a range of mountains bearing the same name and over which we had to cross to reach Colville Valley. The mission we learned was deserted. He concluded to take us upon the payment of a blanket and a shirt. My feet are still very sore. Snowed hard all night.

SATURDAY, MARCH 5, 1859.   Having partaken of a meal of fresh fish we started and soon came to the portage. The unpacking and repacking was soon effected. These canoes are made of birch bark; and a man can carry a very large one with ease. Came to an Indian camp at noon. Here there were several lodges. Stopped at the chief's lodge and had the satisfaction of seeing the remains of 17 deer strung up. They fed us bountifully with venison. Stayed all night here. Here also we found articles that once were owned by our former comrades. These Indians are as punctual in their devotions as the Kutenai, but are by far more warlike in appearance than the latter. Weather pleasant.

SUNDAY MARCH 6, 1859.   Evidently we are out of danger, for my dreams last night were of home and the scenes of my youth. Not a scene of our past journey or the future that lay before us presented itself. I was questioned as usual, but could make no reply but that I thought that we were out of danger as I did not dream of anything concerning the trip.

Started early. We soon came to swift current and rapids and soon reached in close proximity to a fall. We were all fearful (except the Indian) that we were going over, and our minds were in a fearful state for we thought that he could not manage the canoe in such rapids; but when within about twenty feet of the falls and close in to shore by a dexterous movement he moored the canoe into a small bay which was hidden by rocks. Here we effected a landing and made a portage of about two hundred yards. Reloading, we were soon on our way and reached "Old Paul's" encampment late in the afternoon where we were kindly received. Upon unloading the canoe we found that we had left our axe at the portage. The Indian who brought us down seeing our fix gave us his hatchet, and informed us that he would take the axe back with him to which we gladly assented. The scenery on the river today was grand and beautiful, even clothed in [white?], and it must be transcendingly so when clothed in verdure.

We found several families domiciled in Old Paul's lodge; but they made room for us. They were, we found, not so abundantly blessed with provisions as we hoped. During our evening *tete-a-tete* we learned from them further particulars regarding our four comrades. They arrived safe at Spokane River but in a starved state and destitute of clothing.[2] Our conversation is carried on by pantomime; but we have become so thoroughly acquainted with it that it is almost as plain as speaking. Several of the squaws here were also dressed in calico gowns. There was one I noticed particularly. She was much whiter than the balance; and her dress was scrupulously neat and perfectly weighted down with ornaments. I almost fell in love with her. I afterwards learned from white men that she is called Tsa-mah-ku-ke-ola, or "Pride of the Valley." She was by far the prettiest squaw that I have seen from the Gulf of Mexico to the fifty-fourth parallel of north latitude. Had fish and boiled wheat for supper. The wheat they raised.

The old man who brought us down informed us that he had got through with his journey; and that we should now hire another guide to take us over the mountain which lay opposite to us. Acting upon the suggestion we hired a young brave from Old Paul, giving him for his services a blanket, shirt, and an oil cloth bag.

Weather snowing hard. My feet are still very sore; and I dread on that account the trip before me. We have now two blankets left and one shirt apiece which we have on our backs. Both blankets are mine and intended to keep them on account of the selfishness of Palmer all the way through; but now that he is parted with his last blanket, and Houck also, I have given one to Houck, as he was my partner, but still giving Palmer the use of both. Now I am satisfied as I have brought him to terms.

[2] Subsequently Jones learned that the party of four had been kept for four days by this band of Indians and then sent with a guide to the Colville Valley. *Chatfield Democrat,* 18, 25 June 1859; *St. Paul Daily Pioneer and Democrat,* 25 June 1859; *Faribault Central Republican,* 22 June 1859; *Mankato Weekly Independent,* 16 July 1859. See also entry for 9 March 1859 below.

MONDAY, MARCH 7, 1859.   Started early. Crossed the river. Struck across the valley which is of considerable width. Crossed over one range and camped at the foot of the main range. My feet bled very much today and were very painful. Snowed heavy all day and night. Suffered considerably through the night with the cold and snow.

TUESDAY, MARCH 8, 1859.   Commenced the ascent which we found to be more formidable than any we had yet crossed. When nearly to the summit, my strength completely failed; and here I determined my bones should lay. I told Houck and Palmer to go on, never mind me. If I recovered any strength I would endeavor to follow their tracks. I thanked Houck with tears in my eyes for the manly part he had ever acted towards me while on the trip. I then lay down perfectly resigned to my fate, in fact perfectly indifferent whether I should freeze or starve to death. Houck would not leave me, and said if I were going to stay there and meet my fate, he would bear me company. Palmer rested a few moments and started after the guide. He would not take his turn to break the track, although he was by far better abled than I was. After resting for some time, Houck by coaxing and sometimes using force finally succeeded in getting me to the summit where we found the guide and Palmer resting.

The snow on the mountain must be of an immense depth, as only the tops of the trees embedded in snow were to be seen. The air was very cold and invigorating and had a good effect on my exhausted state. We rested here for some time. We vainly scanned the valley for a sight of the Columbia River. We saw no stream, but as far as the eye could reach mountains after mountains reared their snow-clad heads.

The guide, all at once without giving any warning, jumped up as if struck by an arrow and started down the mountain with a speed that defied keeping up with. He was soon lost to sight; and we saw him no more. This is the third time we have been deserted by our guides. There is no dependence whatever to be placed in a guide that is paid beforehand. We started and followed his track. After we had reached the valley, we heard his whoop and responded.

Late in the evening we came across a well-beaten trail which we followed. As soon as we struck it we took off our snowshoes, which afforded me considerable relief. We followed the trail some distance; and as we were crossing a marsh, we saw a man on the opposite side. We hailed him but he took no notice of it. We crossed the marsh in the direction we saw him and entered Colville Valley. As soon as we got through a small neck of timber, we descried houses. We entered one and found it occupied by Indians and a white man, laid up with his feet badly frozen, bearing the sobriquet of "Butcher Brown." So glad were we to see [him] that we almost felt like hugging him. The poor fellow froze his feet the night before and had been brought to the shanty but a short while before our arrival. From him we learned that we were now in Colville Valley and that these Indians were Spokans[3] and were now friendly. They sat us down a large mess of fresh venison, which we went into with a will. Finishing our meal, the squaw prepared some robes and blankets, and we were all soon reveling in happy glee in the halls of dreamland.

[3] While other Indians are referred to hereafter, this is the last band designated specifically. In a notation at the end of his journal Jones listed the "Names of the different tribes we passed. West side [of the Rocky Mountains:] Kutenai, Pen d'Oreilles, Colville, Okanagons, Spokans, Nez Perces, Snakes, Forks, Walla Wallas, Cayuse, Yygh, Umatillahs, Clackamas, Klickitats, Simcoes, Yakimas, Weenatchees."

See notes 17, 19, chapter 14, above. The Wallawalla were closely related to the Nez Perce. The Cayuse had murdered Marcus Whitman and destroyed his mission when smallpox decimated the tribe. When Jones encountered them they were partially merged with the Nez Perce. The Umatilla lived in the area of the juncture of the Umatilla and Columbia rivers. The Clackama lived in the Cascade Mountain area. The Klickitat were well known traders in central Washington. The Simcoe were probably the Simkoe-hlama, a subdivision of the Yakima. The Wenatchee lived in the Yakima River country. Swanton, *Indian Tribes of North America*, pp. 424–425, 447–449, 450–451, 454–455, 457, 474. Identity of the Fork and Yygh remains evasive.

WEDNESDAY, MARCH 9, 1859.   When we were ready to start this morning, the mail train came in under charge of Dr. Bates. Hall of our party accompanying him to Walla Walla. From him we learned that Amesbury was staying with a Frenchman about two miles from this place; Emehiser was still further down, stopping with a man named Brown; Hodgeson had gone to Willamette Valley. Dr. Bates and Hall both advised us not to go farther than Brown's as the Okanagans or Colville Indians were decidedly hostile, and that Hall having had a difficult [time] with one he had to make himself scarce in them quarters. Hall looked fat and hearty.[4] Snowed all day. Arrived at Mr. Perroway's where Amesbury was stopping.

THURSDAY, MARCH 10, 1859.   Stayed with Amesbury all day and night.[5] The half-breed wife in the absence of her lord did not look with an eye of favor upon our stay. Bill had almost given up all hopes of ever seeing us again. They had received our letter and had sent us quite a supply of tobacco. They had also made arrangements to meet us as soon as the snow went off with a supply of flour.

FRIDAY, MARCH 11, 1859.   Within a quarter of a mile from Mr. Brown's house lived Old McFlet who has been in this country for twenty-five years. As we were passing his door, he invited us in suspecting that we were a portion of the company from Minnesota. He told his squaw to set us out some bread and milk. It being the first we had for a number of months, we improved the opportunity by stowing away a large quantity.

   After staying a few moments, we made our way to Brown's

---

[4] "Hall having got into a difficulty with an Indian at Fort Colville, had to run, and he concluded to go to the Willamette Valley and stay there till the troops would march for the valley when the snow should disappear." After that "he will try his fortune at the Ponderay mines." *Faribault Central Republican,* 6 July 1859.

[5] "Amesbury found a place with one of the settlers to work for his board." Ibid.

where we found Emehiser who received us with good old *Dutch* hospitality. He was engaged in making rails for Brown. Mr. Thomas Brown is a native of Selkirk Settlement, and he's slightly tinged with the Indian blood. His wife is a native of Scotland and married him at Red River. Both came with Sinclair's train about four years ago. Mrs. Brown is the only white woman in the valley at the present time. Mr. Brown offered us his shop to batch in. Sold us some flour and furnished us with dishes and cooking utensils.[6] To these worthy couple we cannot thank them too much; and we will ever cherish in grateful remembrance the kindness of these warm hearted people.

Emehiser gave us a narrative of their trials to reach this valley. It appears that after we left them they stayed in camp for two days making their snowshoes. They had found old blazes which they followed till they arrived at Flathead Lake and had made fresh blazes all along from the point of starting. They met with no Indians till they arrived at "Old Paul's" encampment, where they found several lodges, and where they traded all they could spare for provisions. From the Indians they learned the direction which to take.

After they had gained the summit of the mountain they struck off on the ridge in a parallel direction with the valley they saw to their right and in a southwesterly course. They wandered for some time and finally reached the Spokane range of mountains where they struck a trail. Following [it] for some time they finally reached "Spokane Geary's" encampment on Spokane River, having been three days without a morsel to eat. They arrived there on New Year's Eve and just in time to participate in their ceremonies. Their mode of celebrating is similar to that of the Kutenai. They were kept there for four days; and a messenger was sent with them to Colville Valley.

[6] Houck and Jones decided to stay there "until the snow goes off." Jones wrote a letter from here, 20 March 1859, to a friend in Chatfield, Minnesota, summarizing the journey from Fort Edmonton. *Chatfield Democrat,* 2 July 1859, reprinted in *St. Paul Daily Pioneer and Democrat,* 10 July 1859.

Spokane Geary, the head chief of the tribe by that name, was educated at the Catholic Institute at Fort Garry on Red River, hence his name. He talks and writes very good English and French. He is reputed to be very treacherous; but our boys say that they were treated first-rate during their stay with him. Before they were summarily chastised by Col. Wright during the previous summer, the regulars had killed seven hundred and fifty horses that were in a corral. This heavy loss and the burning of their lodges brought them to submission. Since then they have been very friendly.

The Fork and Colville Indians around Fort Colville are disposed to be hostile. The settlers here have to go in bands to the Hudson's Bay Company's mill to get their wheat ground; and even then the Indians will endeavor to rob them, as they are in a starving condition. The settlers have entered a complaint to Col. Wright; and he has promised them assistance as soon as the troops could march in the spring. We live in dread all the time. A great many of the settlers have endeavored to organize themselves and take the matter into their own hands; but they cannot persuade those that are in the Company's service and those that have full-blooded Indian wives to participate, their excuse being, "Oh the Indians won't molest us; we are their friends, have married among them, and have lived among them too long to fear any danger."

The settlers have lost a great number of cattle and horses for the want of feed; this winter they say is the hardest winter that has been known and that the snow has stayed longer than usual. It is no uncommon thing for snow to fall to the depth of three feet in this valley.

The valley contains a population of about eighty families. The valley is about thirty miles long and ranging from a mile to five miles in width. Wheat and oats is the main article produced. Vegetables cannot be depended upon, as they are liable to be frostbitten every month during the spring and summer months. Farmers here have told me that in a field of twenty acres their crop of oats would be killed in spots, and the balance would flourish. I cannot account for this strange phenomenon. I should certainly think that the frost would make a clean sweep and not show any favors. McFlet who lives but a very short distance from Brown's—the lands of both are apparently of the same quality and of the same level. McFlet has tried to raise a crop for four years in succession and failed each time; while on the other hand his neighbor has raised excellent crops. This year McFlet is going to remove his field of operations.

SATURDAY, MARCH 12, 1859.   Houck went to Mr. Perroway and bought a few pounds of fresh beef at 75¢ per pound and a bushel of potatoes at $2.00 per bushel.[7] Snowing all day.

SUNDAY, MARCH 13, 1859.   Cloudy and thawing. Mr. Brown and myself took a sleigh ride for about four miles to Fiddler's Ranch kept by Bob Pelky, a printer who served his time (so he says) in the *St. Louis Republican.* He recently married a full-blooded squaw.

MONDAY, MARCH 14, 1859.   Houck went to the store which is about ten miles distant, bought a few articles of clothing which were very dear. Clear and thawing.

TUESDAY, MARCH 15, 1859.   Clear and thawing. Houck is assisting Emehiser to split rails. My feet are too sore to permit to walk any distance on foot. Most of my toes were cut to the bone.

WEDNESDAY, MARCH 16, 1859.   Clear and thawing.

THURSDAY, MARCH 17, 1859.   Clear and thawing. Took a sleigh ride to Bob Pelky's ranch.

[7] Jones and Houck commented elsewhere that "Groceries and merchandise of every description are pretty high: flour $10 per hundred; ham and pickled pork, 75 cts. per pound; beef, 25 cts.; sugar, 75 cts.; tea $2; coffee 75 cts.; soap $ a bar; clothing in proportion." *Faribault Central Republican,* 6 July 1859.

FRIDAY, MARCH 18, 1859.   Informed John Palmer that he must shift for himself, as we could not afford to keep him any longer. He soon found work. Weather clear and cold.

SATURDAY, MARCH 19, 1859.   Cloudy and thawing.

SUNDAY, MARCH 20, 1859.   Clear and thawing.

MONDAY, MARCH 21, 1859.   Mild. Snowed three inches. Mrs. McFlet made us a pair of moccasins apiece with sole leather bottoms.

TUESDAY, MARCH 22, 1859.   Cloudy and thawing. Traded off a silver watch which was worthless for $30 in trade.

WEDNESDAY, MARCH 23, 1859.   Clear and thawing. Occupied the time in writing letters home.

THURSDAY, MARCH 24, 1859.   Rain throughout day and night. Wrote letters.

FRIDAY, MARCH 25, 1859.   Clear and thawing.

SATURDAY, MARCH 26, 1859.   Clear and thawing.

SUNDAY, MARCH 27, 1859.   Clear and thawing.

MONDAY, MARCH 28, 1859.   Cloudy and thawing.

TUESDAY, MARCH 29, 1859.   Rain and thawing.

WEDNESDAY, MARCH 30, 1859.   Rain and thawing. Snow fast disappearing.

THURSDAY, MARCH 31, 1859.   Cloudy and cold.

FRIDAY, APRIL 1, 1859.   Clear and mild.

SATURDAY, APRIL 2, 1859.   Palmer has gone to work for the Hudson's Bay Company. Weather mild and thawing.

SUNDAY, APRIL 3, 1859.   Clear and thawing.

MONDAY, APRIL 4, 1859.   Clear and thawing.

TUESDAY, APRIL 5, 1859.   Clear and thawing.

WEDNESDAY, APRIL 6, 1859.   Rode to the store. My feet are getting nearly well. Clear and thawing.

THURSDAY, APRIL 7, 1859.   A young man named Richard Fry has just come in from the Pend Oreille mines. He is on his way to the Willamette Valley to visit his parents. He has been at the mines for two years, and only brings with him about $700 worth of dust.[8] Weather clear and thawing.

FRIDAY, APRIL 8, 1859.   Clear and thawing.

SATURDAY, APRIL 9, 1859.   Clear and thawing.

SUNDAY, APRIL 10, 1859.   Occupied the day in baking hard bread. Having come to the conclusion that I should go to The Dalles. Houck has got a job of building a house and will stay.

MONDAY, APRIL 11, 1859.   Hired a mule which was stole from some military post, from Tom Brown, the only animal I could get, for which I had to pay $25. We bid farewell to Brown and his family, Houck and Emehiser, and started in company with young Fry.

TUESDAY, APRIL 12, 1859.   Found the snow too deep on the right-hand side of the creek, and concluded to return to Brown's and try the left-hand road. On our way back we mired several times. Weather warm and thawing.

WEDNESDAY, APRIL 13, 1859.   Again started and soon caught up with Houston's train who are bound for The Dalles.[9]

[8] In this connection, in their letter of 25 March 1859, Jones and Houck commented that "News has been received from the Fraser river mines, that a great number of the miners have died from starvation; Indians too sharing the same fate. The mines are very rich they say, so far exceeding California in her palmiest days. The Ponderay mines, which are about 40 miles from here, they say are far richer than California if they could turn the river, which they are talking of doing." Ibid.

[9] They were following the Colville Road which went due south to Walla Walla

Camped at the mouth of the valley about a mile from the Indian dwellings. Had to cross our baggage in a canoe, as the stream was very high. Weather warm and thawing. We have joined messes. There are five of us altogether.

THURSDAY, APRIL 14, 1859.   Before leaving camp, a Mexican train came into camp. They are on their way to Fraser River. Camped at night on Prairie Du Mort, or Dead Man's Prairie—the name arising from the fact that two men had died on this prairie from eating poison kamus.[10]

FRIDAY, APRIL 15, 1859.   Camped on Walker's Prairie. No snow in the valley. Snow on the hills.

SATURDAY, APRIL 16, 1859.   Passed Walker's Mission (now deserted) soon after leaving camp. Met Lafleur and Robert's trains bound for Colville and Fraser River.[11] Arrived at Spokane River. Saw Dr. Bates from whom we procured a mess of fresh horse meat. Camped at Little Creek.

SUNDAY, APRIL 17, 1859.   After passing Little Creek we came to open and rough country. Camped at Rock Creek. No snow. Few bushes along the creek.

MONDAY, APRIL 18, 1859.   Camped at Big Lake.[12] Passed the battleground late in the afternoon. We met with no snow today. Crossed several tracts strongly impregnated with alkali.

and down the Walla Walla River to the Columbia River. Otis W. Freeman, "Early Wagon Roads in the Inland Empire," *Pacific Northwest Quarterly* 45 (October 1954): 125–130. See especially map page 127.

[10] Probably death camas, a common plant, the bulb of which is poisonous. The bulb of another variety of camas was a staple food and trade item for some Indian tribes. Douglas Leechman, "Camas—A Sumptuous Feast," *Beaver* Outfit 303 (Summer 1972): 4–6.

[11] The Colville Road was the trail followed by Indians, missionaries, miners, and others who were bound from the Snake and Columbia rivers for the Colville Valley and Canada. Freeman, "Early Wagon Roads in the Inland Empire," p. 125.

[12] Big Lake is now called Colville Lake or Sprague Lake. Ibid., p. 126.

TUESDAY, APRIL 19, 1859.   Camped at Cow Creek. Here we met the Hudson's Bay Company's train also encamped bound for Colville. Some small willows along the creek. Our provision is all gone.

WEDNESDAY, APRIL 20, 1859.   This afternoon we went off the road to visit Palouse Falls. Palouse River at this place runs through a gorge; the sides are perpendicular and has the appearance of being chiseled. These cliffs rise upwards of two hundred feet on either side. The falls are perpendicular and as near as I should judge two hundred feet. From the foot of the falls the cliffs also rise perpendicular on either side. Camped at the mouth of Palouse River near its junction with Snake River. There is an Indian encampment on the opposite side. Saw Fort Taylor in the distance.

THURSDAY, APRIL 21, 1859.   Camped on Touchet River, a small stream. Passed considerable acid and alkaline lands. There is no water between Snake and Touchet Rivers. Distance 35 miles.

FRIDAY, APRIL 22, 1859.   One of Houston's half-breeds and young Fry left this morning to go to New Fort Walla Walla. We proceed to old Fort Walla [Walla] on the Columbia River.[13] Character of the country rolling, sandy, and covered with sage brush and cactus. Saw numerous horned frogs. No water between Touchet and the Columbia.

SATURDAY, APRIL 23, 1859.   Crossed Walla Walla River and camped on the banks of the Columbia. Trail very rough and rocky.

SUNDAY, APRIL 24, 1859.   Some of our horses are missing. Spent nearly all day in looking for them but to no use. We only made about six miles today. Late in the evening the

---

[13] Fort Walla Walla was located where the Walla Walla River joins the Columbia River at present Wallula. It was abandoned and replaced in 1857 by another fort situated up river at present Walla Walla. Ibid., pp. 125–126.

"Greaser," who joined us at Spokane River, came in and reported that he had tracked them to an island; but as it was too dark he wouldn't drive them up.

MONDAY, APRIL 25, 1859.   Houston and the Greaser, as soon as we were opposite the island, went over. The river was very shallow at this point. They found the horses and an Indian herding them. The Indian had driven [them] in a circuitous route over the prairie and then to the island. He was a frightened Indian. When he saw he was caught, we had a notion of *swinging* him; but on a second consideration we considered it punishment enough to take his horse. Camped on the banks of the Umatilla River. Crossed our goods in a canoe. Indian camp on the opposite side.

TUESDAY, APRIL 26, 1859.   Camped near Willow Creek. Two deserters from Walla Walla came in after dark. Trail very rough and rocky.

WEDNESDAY, APRIL 27, 1859.   Camped near John Day River. Saw Mount Hood for the first time. Trail very rough.

THURSDAY, APRIL 28, 1859.   Camped at Deschutes River. At this place we found a good bridge, store, and half dozen houses in addition to the old block fort.

FRIDAY, APRIL 29, 1859.   Arrived at The Dalles at noon. While marching down the street, I saw a group of U.S. Officers. They saw the U.S. brand on the mule and ordered me to stop. Capt. Jordan (so I afterwards learned) inquired of me of whom and where I got the mule. I answered that I got him from Colville but declined giving the individual's name. He said that he would have to claim him, to which I readily assented as he was not worth a continental. He intimated that the mule was stolen; and I concurred in his opinion. As I would not give him the name of the person of whom I hired the mule, he said I was liable to be prosecuted, to which opinion I thought as he did and intimated to him that nothing would afford me greater pleasure than to live awhile at someone's expense, as it was the first civilized spot that I stepped my foot in for nearly a year.

On the following day I got work and was agreeably surprised to find that Capt. Jordan was one of my *bosses* and to whom I had to look for the needful. The captain read with interest my journal and published a portion, as [he] also noticed the arrival of one of the pioneer party to this country by the way of British America.[14]

List of the Pioneer party that Crossed the Mountains.

J. L. Houck	Faribault, Minnesota.
J. E. Smith	Faribault, Minnesota.
J. W. Jones	Faribault, Minnesota.
J. Palmer	Faribault, Minnesota.
I. Emehiser	Faribault, Minnesota.
W. Amesbury	Faribault, Minnesota.
J. Schaeffter	Faribault, Minnesota.
J. Gibson	Woodville, Minnesota.
J. J. Hall	Mankato, Minnesota.
G. W. Hodgeson	Mankato, Minnesota.

REMARKS   The route from St. Paul, Minn., to Pembina cannot be depended on for game along the road. Early in the

[14] Published in *The Dalles Journal,* 6 May 1859. The synopsis is reprinted in *Chatfield Democrat,* 18, 25 June 1859; *St. Paul Daily Pioneer and Democrat,* 25 June 1859; *Faribault Central Republican,* 22 June 1859; *Mankato Weekly Independent,* 16 July 1859. The St. Paul and Mankato papers mistakenly referred to it as *The Dalles Herald.* Captain Thomas Jordan, commander at Fort Dalles, began publication of *The Dalles Journal* in early 1859 but sold it within the year, when its name was changed to *The Dalles Mountaineer.* George S. Turnbull, *History of Oregon Newspapers* (Portland, Oreg.: Binfords & Mort, 1939), p. 137.

No files of *The Dalles Journal* have ever been found. As noted above, it was quoted in the Minnesota newspapers, possibly from copies sent back by Jones. The Jones account was also noted in regional newspapers. The *Victoria Gazette,* 9 June 1859, for example, reported its appearance in The Dalles paper via the *Olympia* (Wash. Territory) *Pioneer and Democrat,* no date given.

spring the lakes will afford fowl, but as for buffalo, elk, and deer, cannot be had but by an experienced hunter. After leaving Lake George by the west trail, you will find but little timber. And for three days none whatever. Distance from St. Paul to Pembina 456 miles. From Pembina to Fort Garry the country is low and marshy with small groves. Distance [65 miles]. The greater portion of the country between Fort Garry and Fort Ellice on the Assinniboine River is marshy, the latter half with numerous lakes, and where waterfowl may be had in abundance.

From Fort Ellice to Touchwood Hills the country is similar for the first half. The last is noted for its alkaline and saline lakes. For three days we had to pack wood with us.

From Touchwood to Carlton the country is more rough with numerous lakes of fresh, alkaline, and saline lakes. Water fowl may be had in abundance.

From Carlton to Pitt the country is diversified but still dotted with numerous lakes. Wood and water plenty.

From Fort Pitt to Edmonton the country is rough to within three days travel of Edmonton when it changes to a willow swamp. Between these two places we saw the first buffalo since leaving Minnesota. Wood, water, game of all kind in abundance. The distance from Fort Garry as measured by Goodrich and Smith's odometer is 716 miles by the nearest route; but by the one we followed it is much more. We had no odometer with us, as we had left Smith and Goodrich at Pembina.[15]

From Edmonton to the mouth of the Kootenay Pass, Capt. Blakiston estimates it at 300 miles almost due south. The country is similar to that between Ft. Pitt and Edmonton till within three days' march of the mountains, when it becomes mountainous.

From the Kootenay Pass to Colville I estimate it at the least

[15] Goodrich and Smith arrived at The Dalles, 31 August. See note 29, chapter 1, above.

calculation 450 miles. The country is nothing but a succession of mountains and valleys. Game is exceedingly scarce; and no one should attempt to travel from these two points without taking enough supply of provisions to last them through.

From Colville to The Dalles is, if my memory serves me right, 464 miles. From Spokane River you leave the mountains and enter a barren plain with some few fertile spots. The country as a general thing is sandy and rocky.

DISTANCES BY GOODRICH'S ODOMETER

From St. Paul to Pembina	466
From Pembina to Ft. Garry	70
From Ft. Garry to Ft. Ellice	231
From Ft. Ellice to Touchwood Hills	169
From Touchwood to South Branch of Saskatchewan	129
From South to North Branch of Saskatchewan	55
From North Saskatchewan to Ft. Pitt	175
From Ft. Pitt to Edmonton	180

BIBLIOGRAPHY

MANUSCRIPTS

Hudson's Bay Company Archives, Provincial Archives of Manitoba, Winnipeg.
  B.60/a/30. Edmonton Post Journal, 1858–1860.
  B.63/a/4. Fort Ellice Post Journal, 1858–1859 [1864].
  B.235/a/16. Winnipeg Post Journal, 1858–1860.

Bureau of the Census. United States Department of Commerce. National Archives, Washington, D.C.
  Record Group 29. Microfilm roll 367. Seventh Census of the United States, 1850. Minnesota Territory.
  Record Group 29. Microfilm roll 1056. Eighth Census of the United States, 1860. Multnomah County, Wasco County, Oregon.
  Record Group 29. Microfilm roll 834. Ninth Census of the United States, 1870. Lander County, Nevada.

Provincial Archives of British Columbia, Victoria.
  William Brewster Correspondence Outward.

MAPS

Canada. Department of Energy, Mines and Resources. Topographic Maps.
  Banff-Bassano. 1:500 000
  Brandon-Winnipeg. 1:500 000
  Broadview-Dauphin. 1:500 000
  Cranbrook-Lethbridge. 1:500 000
  Indian Head-Brandon. 1:500 000
  Moose Jaw-Watrous. 1:500 000

Okanagan-Kootenay. 1:500 000
Red Deer-Edmonton. 1:500 000
Saskatoon-Prince Albert. 1:500 000
Wainwright-Battleford. 1:500 000

United States. Department of the Interior. Geological Survey. Topographic
Maps.
Idaho. 1:500 000
Minnesota. 1:500 000
Montana. 1:500 000
North Dakota. 1:500 000
Washington. 1:500 000

NEWSPAPERS

Chatfield (Minn.) *Democrat.*
Daily Reese River (Austin, Nev.) *Reveille.*
Faribault (Minn.) *Central Republican.*
Mankato (Minn.) *Weekly Independent.*
Montreal (Quebec) *Argus.*
Saint Paul (Minn.) *Daily Minnesotian.*
St. Paul (Minn.) *Daily Pioneer and Democrat.*
Saint Paul (Minn.) *Weekly Minnesotian.*
The Dalles (Oreg.) *Journal.*
Toronto (Ontario) *Globe.*
Victoria (British Columbia) *Gazette.*

BOOKS AND ARTICLES

Ackermann, Gertrude W., ed. "An Optimistic Pioneer in a Period of Depres-
sion." *Minnesota History* 13 (June 1932): 174–178.
Ball, Robert Stawell. *A Popular Guide to the Heavens: A Series of Eighty-Six
Plates with Explanatory Text and Index.* 4th ed. London: George Philip &
Son, 1925.
Dictionary of Canadian Biography.
S.v. "De Smet, Pierre-Jean," by William L. Davis.
S.v. "McTavish, William," by N. Jaye Goossen.
S.v. "Palliser, John," by Irene M. Spry.
Freeman, Otis W. "Early Wagon Roads in the Inland Empire." *Pacific North-
west Quarterly* 45 (October 1954): 125–130.
Galbraith, John S. *The Little Emperor: Governor Simpson of the Hudson's
Bay Company.* Toronto: Macmillan of Canada, 1976.
Gilman, Rhoda R.; Gilman, Carolyn; and Stultz, Deborah M. *The Red River
Trails: Oxcart Routes Between St. Paul and the Selkirk Settlement, 1820–
1870.* St. Paul: Minnesota Historical Society, 1979.

Giraud, Marcel. *The Metis in the Canadian West.* 2 vols. Translated by George Woodcock. Lincoln: University of Nebraska Press, 1986.

Gluek, Alvin C., Jr. *Minnesota and the Manifest Destiny of the Canadian Northwest: A Study in Canadian American Relations.* Toronto: University of Toronto Press, 1965.

————. "The Minnesota Route." *Beaver* Outfit 286 (Spring 1956): 44–50.

Hodge, Frederick Webb, ed. *Handbook of American Indians North of Mexico.* Bureau of American Ethnology, Bulletin 30. 2 vols. Washington: Government Printing Office, 1907–1910.

Howay, Frederic W. *The Early History of the Fraser River Mines.* Archives of British Columbia, Memoir No. 6. Victoria: Provincial Library, 1926.

Kelly, J. Wells, comp. *First Directory of Nevada Territory, Containing the Names of Residents in the Principal Towns; A Historical Sketch, the Organic Act, and Other Political Matters of Interest; Together with a Description of All the Quartz Mills; Reduction Works, and All Other Industrial Establishments in the Territory; as Also of the Leading Mining Claims.* San Francisco: Valentine & Co., 1862.

————, comp. *Second Directory of Nevada Territory; Embracing a General Directory of Residents of all Principal Towns; Business Directory of Advertisers, Quartz Mills, Reduction Works, Toll Roads, Etc.* Virginia [City], Nev.: Printed by Valentine & Co., 1863.

Klinck, Carl F.; Bailey, Alfred G.; Bissell, Claude; Daniells, Roy; Frye, Northrop; and Pacey, Desmond, eds. *Literary History of Canada: Canadian Literature in English.* 3 vols. 2d ed. Toronto: University of Toronto Press, 1976.

Lass, William E. *Minnesota's Boundary with Canada: Its Evolution since 1783.* St. Paul: Minnesota Historical Society Press, 1980.

Leechman, Douglas. "Camas—A Sumptuous Feast." *Beaver* Outfit 303 (Summer 1972): 4–6.

Lent, D. Geneva. *West of the Mountains: James Sinclair and the Hudson's Bay Company.* Seattle: University of Washington Press, 1963.

McMicking, Thomas. *Overland from Canada to British Columbia. By Mr. Thomas McMicking of Queenston, Canada West.* Edited by Joanne Leduc. Vancouver: University of British Columbia Press, 1981.

McNaughton, Margaret. *Overland to Cariboo: An Eventful Journey of Canadian Pioneers to the Gold Fields of British Columbia in 1862.* Introduction by Victor G. Hopwood. Vancouver: J. J. Douglas, 1973.

Marcy, Randolph B. *Exploration of the Red River of Louisiana, in the Year 1852.* 32d Cong., 2d sess., Senate, Executive Doc. No. 54, Serial 666, 1853.

Minnesota Legislature. House. Select Committee on Overland Route to British Oregon. Report. 1st Leg., 1st sess., 1858.

Morton, Arthur S. *A History of the Canadian West to 1870–71: Being a History of Rupert's Land (The Hudson's Bay Company's Territory) and of the*

North-west Territory (Including the Pacific Slope). 2d ed. Edited by Lewis G. Thomas. Toronto: Published in Cooperation with University of Saskatchewan by University of Toronto Press, 1973.

──────. *Sir George Simpson, Overseas Governor of the Hudson's Bay Company: A Pen Picture of a Man of Action*. [Portland]: Published by Binsford-Mart for the Oregon Historical Society, 1944.

Ormsby, Margaret A. *British Columbia: A History*. Toronto: The Macmillans in Canada, 1958.

Russell, Ralph C. "The Carlton Trail." *Saskatchewan History* 8 (Winter 1955): 22–27.

──────. *The Carlton Trail: The Broad Highway into the Saskatchewan Country from the Red River Settlement, 1840–1880*. Rev. ed. Saskatoon, Saskatchewan: Modern Press, 1956.

Spry, Irene M. *The Palliser Expedition: An Account of John Palliser's British North American Expedition, 1857–1860*. Toronto: Macmillan Co. of Canada, 1963.

──────, ed. *The Papers of the Palliser Expedition, 1857–1860*. Publications of the Champlain Society, vol. 44. Toronto: Champlain Society, 1968.

──────. "Routes through the Rockies: Palliser's Precursors in the Passes Leading through the Rocky Mountains from the Headwaters of the Saskatchewan River." *Beaver* Outfit 294 (Autumn 1963): 26–39.

Storm, Colton, comp. *A Catalogue of the Everett D. Graff Collection of Western Americana*. Chicago: Published for The Newberry Library by University of Chicago Press, 1968.

Swanton, John R. *The Indian Tribes of North America*. Bureau of American Ethnology, Bulletin 145. Washington: Government Printing Office, 1952.

[Thompson, Thomas H., and West, Albert A.] *Reproduction of Thompson and West's History of Nevada. 1881. With Illustrations and Biographical Sketches of Its Prominent Men and Pioneers*. Introduction by David F. Myrick. Berkeley, California: Howell-North, 1958.

Turnbull, George S. *History of Oregon Newspapers*. Portland, Oreg.: Binfords & Mort, 1939.

Van Kirk, Sylvia. *Many Tender Ties: Women in Fur-Trade Society, 1670–1870*. 1st American ed. Norman: University of Oklahoma Press, 1983.

Wade, Mark Sweeten. *The Overlanders of '62*. Archives of British Columbia, no. 9. Victoria: Printed by Charles F. Banfield, 1931.

Wallace, W. Stewart. *The Dictionary of Canadian Biography*. 2d ed., 2 vols. Toronto: Macmillan Co., 1945.

Whipple, Fred L. "The Rotation of Comet Nuclei." In *Comets*, 227–250. Edited by Laurel L. Wilkening. Tucson: University of Arizona Press, 1982.

INDEX

A NOTE ABOUT THE AUTHOR

Dwight L. Smith is Professor Emeritus of history at Miami University. He is currently investigating British naval surveillance in the Canadian Pacific Northwest coastal waters in the 1860s.

$\dfrac{26^{95}}{15^{00}}$